The
Deckchair
Gardener

Also by Anne Wareham

Outwitting Squirrels: and Other Garden Pests
and Nuisances

The Deckchair Gardener

An Improper Gardening Manual

ANNE WAREHAM

MICHAEL O'MARA BOOKS LIMITED

*Especially for those who love gardens
and hate gardening.*

First published in Great Britain in 2017 by
Michael O'Mara Books Limited
9 Lion Yard
Tremadoc Road
London SW4 7NQ

A CIP catalogue record for this book is available from the British Library.

Papers used by Michael O'Mara Books Limited are natural, recyclable products made from wood grown in sustainable forests. The manufacturing processes conform to the environmental regulations of the country of origin.

ISBN: 978-1-78243-642-3 in paperback print format
ISBN: 978-1-78243-643-0 in ebook format

2 3 4 5 6 7 8 9 10
Illustrations by Kate Charlesworth
Designed and typeset by K. DESIGN, Winscombe, Somerset

Printed and bound by CPI Group (UK) Ltd, Croydon, CR0 4YY

www.mombooks.com

Contents

Introduction

It's not nice to be called lazy, but as we live in a world where long working hours and hectic schedules are the exhausting norm for many of us, we do need to take it easy sometimes. When we finally have some spare time, we often find ourselves too decrepit and fed up to spend it feeding, mowing, seeding, scarifying, de-mossing and weeding the lawn. Generally, for a great many of us caring for a demanding garden is just too much. But if you have managed to acquire a house or ground-floor flat in this country, you are likely to have such a monster outside, practically yelling for attention. And you may possibly have critical neighbours peering at the muddy mess and thinking bad thoughts about you. Or so you fear.

So this book is not addressed to the keen gardener, though I hope they will also find treasure within. It's principally addressed to you, the much-neglected reluctant gardener. You don't watch the TV gardening shows longing to know how to grow a cucumber, and you never touch gardening magazines because they bring on a severe bout of depression. You may be reluctant because you hate the outdoors and hate gardening outdoors most of all. Maybe the garden is just too big, or you'd love a beautiful garden but there's no way you want outdoor housework added to your list of chores. Or you'd love a beautiful garden and already have the plot, but you have no idea of how to turn the plot into said garden before you're dead or bankrupt. Maybe you do have a beautiful garden already but – here the keen gardener *does* slip in – the way you have been looking after it is just impossible to continue. So, I want to help.

It's important for me to say at this point that probably the most important thing I can offer you is not so much alternative ways of gardening – though I do have a lot of those for you – but perhaps a different mindset. A mindset that involves asking yourself 'Do I *have* to?' whenever you are faced with something you don't like doing. Followed by 'Might there be another way?' when you decide it's just a horrible way to spend your time.

At Veddw House, I was originally faced with what

rapidly proved to be an impossible task: to create a garden out of two fields, with a spade and very little money or help, and at a time when I was not even very well. I had to find alternative ways of doing things – and I did. I thought I might have to dig everywhere I wanted to make a border, and I even made a feeble effort in that direction. But that really seemed a bit too much like hard work, so I researched hard for alternatives, and discovered mulching. This involves covering the soil or, in this case, grass, with organic matter, which cuts out the light to whatever is growing underneath and kills it. For initial land clearing it takes about 15 to 20 cm (6–8 in) of something like bark or wood chippings, thereafter about 5 cm (2 in). The soil is fed by the rotting vegetation and the mulch itself (there is no significant nitrogen depletion, no matter what people say, quite the opposite). The mulch benefits the soil also by adding humus – this is not the stuff you eat as a dip with flat bread, which is hummus. Don't eat soil, however well mulched – it's gritty. Thanks to mulching, a two-acre ornamental garden suddenly became possible. Instead of digging, I mulched where I wanted beds and borders. (You can see something of the result on our website veddw.com.)

I also had no idea of how to separate a grass path from a border with no money to pay for edgings, and had no inclination to do the edgings myself. Observation led me to plants like *Alchemilla mollis*, which kindly keeps edges for me. To level a piece of ground I needed a retaining wall, which we all know costs the earth. Instead, I planted two beech hedges with earth-retaining roots. One to hold back the soil and one in front to hide the soil and root. They have supported that bank through all weathers for over twenty years. And so I went on, problem solving all the way.

So part of my intention here is to encourage you, whether you have several acres or a little roof garden, to risk experimenting and finding new and easier ways to do things. Be sceptical about what I say, and be sceptical about every bit of garden advice you are offered. There may yet be an easier way – and that way lies revolution and, potentially, relaxation.

How to be a deckchair gardener

If you know *anything* about gardening, this will not be easy. If you want to take it easy outside, it's best if you know nothing about gardening. That way you will have much less to unlearn. Unlearning is hard. Science says so – never mind your own experience of making New Year's resolutions. Science has experimented with giving mice a sugar craving and then comparing what happens to the brains of the mice with a sweet tooth to the brains of the mice without when it comes to pressing a button for a sugar treat. Without getting too technical here, the mice with the sugar habit had such obvious and dramatic brain change that (Warning: sensitive souls, look away now) it was possible to tell which ones they were just from looking at separated bits of their brain in a Petri dish. So your gardening habits – while no one is suggesting that they are sugar sweet – are etched into your brain, and if you've been a conscientious and concerned gardener all your life, even if your life has so far been a short one, you will have some serious unlearning to do. It can't be easy to rearrange your brain, can it?

In fact, it's not easy to become laid-back about anything once you have absorbed the lessons many of us are taught as children. Typically, we may be taught from an early age to keep busy and to do things 'properly', and both these things militate against being a good layabout. It sounds on the surface as if being lazy would be easy (lazy has that kind of reputation). But it isn't, so learning to take it easy will actually be your first and most serious task if you are, as it were, to be properly laid-back.

Then there's all the specific gardening learning you may be burdened with, such as how to be a 'good' gardener. You may have worked hard at that one while you sat in front of the telly with a glass of wine or two, wondering how Monty Don does all that with just two dogs to help him. You might even have embarked on your gardening education back when Geoff Hamilton was creating lots of jobs for you, like the eternal 'how to take a cutting'. That one never made sense to me, though it's a popular one, since what most people like in their gardens is a plethora of random and different plants. What do they do with all their successful cuttings? Start a nursery, I suppose, and therein lies much grief. Stick with the day job, especially if it has a pension.

The 'proper' vs the 'improper' gardener

Even a total novice gardener may have admired the tidy and busy gardens of those 'proper gardeners' and this in itself will have left you with a lot to unlearn. You may also have got the parental and TV gardeners' rules confused and become a gardening parent: it is currently the thing to drag small children away from happy times with their computers out into the cold and wet to learn to become good citizen gardeners and to have fun. 'Fun' is an ominous term and we should all learn as soon as possible to avoid all threats of having fun. I understand Shakespeare never knew the word and if he could manage without it we certainly can. It usually turns out to be energetic and hard work. It means you're required to smile and look jolly while you're about it and that, as we all know, is excruciating.

It's hard, unless born naturally to the role, to become a rebel and to be prepared to chuck out all these well-learned rules. You are obviously a good and nice person, reluctant to be difficult, so experimenting and doing things differently comes hard. You will need lots of practice and lots of forgiving yourself when you backslide and find yourself outside with an edging tool in hand. But you can bolster your resolve with that old line 'practice makes perfect', wander indoors and put the edging tool on eBay.

Part of the difficulty of learning easier techniques is that things will initially look wrong and unfamiliar. And people will arrive and suck their teeth (I've never actually come across anyone sucking their teeth, but I understand that it is an essential component of judicious disapproval) and ask what on earth you are doing *there*. Or *here*, depending. If you are not happy to say that you are experimenting with a different way of doing something, you may need to be creative and find a good lie about how you're doing it for the dog's benefit, or because your back hurts when you bend down. As it surely will should you do anything so foolish.

You will also need to learn to take advice. Most of us are totally unable to do this and hate the very idea. If you don't believe me, try suggesting a different way of loading the dishwasher to your partner. You might as well pack your bags before even attempting it. Indeed, you could even make some money. It will take a bet: I was sitting with some friends once and had just commented that no one takes gardening advice, when someone else approached for a chat – and told us his current garden problem. So I kindly offered a solution, to be met with a blank stare and swift change of subject. Now if I had put a bet on that . . . Try it. Never fails.

So if you are to learn to take advice, you need to be aware of your own propensity to do a little casual laugh and suggest such advice only applies or is useful to other people – who are idiots. Or notice your tendency to hold your breath while someone is giving you their brilliant, life-changing advice. You can always tell when someone isn't listening to you because they will be holding their breath, waiting to retaliate as soon as you have run out of breath. They then, of course, launch into their explanation about why they always do it *this* way. Worse still may be your readiness to tell the advice-giver to shut up and leave you alone. If you tend in that direction, you'd best immediately stop turning down the corner of the pages to keep your place in this book – you need to keep it pristine so you can give it to your best friend for Christmas.

Accept the challenge and be brave

You will now have to learn to give up doing things you have believed were totally essential. Perhaps, worst of all, is knowing the results will be under scrutiny, the garden being quite a public space to be trying all this in. An allotment is the very worst, unless you are very elderly and can pretend, with an authoritative air, when responding to the Allotment Judge that 'people always *used* to do it this way'. That tends to shut most people up unless they are even older than you and know for certain it's a lie.

So how are you going to tackle this challenge if you haven't already cried off and chucked this book in the bin? Well, your first task is to have this awareness – that it's going to be a challenge. Then secondly, it needs to be a challenge you are willing to embrace. And you will need a lot of support and encouragement after that.

If the change of practice involves stopping doing something altogether, you may find it hard to just stop, go indoors and stare at the ceiling. You may need to provide a good explanation for your sudden cessation of activity to a startled partner, in which case ceiling contemplation is unlikely to help.

So you may well need a few good substitute activities for those gardening chores. Playing Candy Crush is a good one, I am told. Cleaning behind the fridge might do. Anything sufficiently distracting. The fridge one has the virtue of worthiness and that is always pleasing to a lazy newbie, especially for the benefit of a bemused partner.

Another tip is to make these changes in small doses – don't try and alter all your garden habits in one go. Just try doing one thing differently this year, and see how that goes. We all know from the sad end of our earlier resolutions that it may be best to take it slowly and cautiously.

You must also learn to distrust yourself. We have lots of lies up our sleeves to justify our being stubborn or daft: 'My dad always did it like this', or 'The worms like it best this way'. Worst of all may be: 'I *like* getting exhausted and bad-tempered for no good reason'. Give it up. Recognize that you are deluding just yourself and that life's too short.

The next thing that will be problematic is that you may have to learn to be brave. Some suggestions in this book could involve clearing the whole garden and starting again. (We'll consider the easiest ways to do this once you have geared yourself up to even think of such a thing.) You can start summoning the courage by imagining clearing the whole garden and rehearsing why you couldn't do it. Then picture clearing a little bit of it and decide you could *possibly* do that instead.

You might need to take on your partner or your children if you want to make your life in the garden better. This might be tricky. They are likely to be hard to persuade and will argue with you about it. Consider enforcing a rule whereby the person who looks after a bit of garden gets to decide what happens in that bit, though you may decide this should only to apply to people over, say, seven.

If you are not brave enough for any of this yet, you might end up believing that it's impossible for you to learn to slob about. But practice and adopting maybe just one of the suggestions in this book might help nudge you in the right direction.

Go your own way

It's very hard to imagine a garden you've never seen before. We tend to base our idea of what a garden is by what our parents did, what our neighbours do and maybe what confronted you when you moved into your place. You might have seen pictures, television programmes, even show gardens at Chelsea or worse. Your own, easier-to-manage garden will be nothing like these and may seem totally weird at first.

Being a sensible human being, you know you should never have taken any of those other gardens seriously, especially as they didn't seem to have a washing line, a demented dog or small children playing football in them. You need to get it clear in your head that those were fantasy gardens as far as you are concerned, just as the clothes you see in fashion magazines are all clearly designed for someone else.

So, you decide to ignore previous gardening models, go your own way and experiment. Hmm. One of the most important things you must do in order to begin making gardening easier is to face up to who *you* are and what you are really like.

For example, I learned that I can make the house tidier by giving myself the odd inflexible rule. Like *never* take any clothes off without next putting them away or in the wash. Ever. (Discourages you from taking a lover, that one.) Once I'd resolved to do this, I found it was easy. It seems I'm like that: I can follow a rule, as long as it's simple, satisfying, easy and often. So it's good for me to build on that and find simple rules that will make my life easier, then stick to them like mad. We've just tidied the potting shed. Time to resolve to *always* put everything away before locking up. Worth a try? Yes, for me. It might just drive you mad. You may prefer to be sloppy and then have a great big annual clear up. Or move house. So *your* approach has to be different, to suit your peculiarities.

If you love mowing the lawn, have a lawn. If you hate mowing, get rid of all grass. If you really do like weeding, then don't mulch – let the weeds come and don't worry about them. They're your treat: you're saving them up for a weeding orgy. If you hate deadheading, give it up and go out occasionally with a hedge trimmer instead. If you long to do nothing else than go out with a wooden trug and carefully remove dying flowers and place them elegantly in your trug, then you must grow things that go over badly and need your expert deadheading skills in order to look fit to live.

So – time to reflect: what do you really, really hate doing out there? Now think about how to get rid of that job forever.

And what do you like? That's the thing to focus on. If it's nothing, you need one of the very minimal-effort suggestions. Read on.

DECKCHAIR WISDOM

It's very hard learning to make things easy: be prepared to struggle. You can take it very slowly, one thing at a time, to make it slightly easier.

To help, give up all magazines, newspaper columns and television programmes on gardening.

STARTING A NEW GARDEN

When we start out, we usually find ourselves lumbered with someone else's garden, and then approach this with a view that plants are pets without legs and so must be treasured whether we like them or not. And most of us are far too impatient to follow the worn old advice to 'wait a year and see what comes up'.

All of that results in a dull, boring garden, and almost inevitably more hard work than necessary. In this case, the first thing to take on board is ruthlessness. Unless you have inherited the garden of a gardener known for growing very special plants (and even then train a very sceptical eye on whatever emerges), regard the plants as dispensable. You could, if it is possible, ask the previous owner whether there is any special treat in store that might be worth waiting to assess. If you like what that is, fair enough, propagate it – your garden will always look better if you are generous and repeat good plants.

If you find shrubs you don't like much, get rid of them. The easiest way to do this is to cut them down to the ground and get rid of the branches in a delectable bonfire, or if you are not permitted that pleasure, take a trip to the dump. You will then need to apply stump killer – no doubt several times – to kill off the remains, since you are not likely to dig it up (too much hard work). But patience – it *will* go and you *will* have new space to use. While you wait, you'll be able to imagine what you might like to have in its place. One of the problems of inheriting a garden is that it deadens the imagination: it's very hard to see beyond what is already there and to imagine alternatives. Getting rid of things helps eliminate this effect and lets you focus on what you might enjoy instead.

Design your garden

This will now leave you with a little garden designing to do. It's worth considering using either straight lines or parts of circles to create your layout. These avoid unpleasant wiggles and are much more pleasing to the eye. Think pattern, play with pattern – and keep it simple. Visit lots of gardens to see what you like and don't like, avoiding getting too preoccupied with the plants while you're learning about layout.

Alternatively, you may actually have a new garden consisting of a field or other 'empty' (empty of garden) space. It happens. It happened to me and quite a few of my friends – it comes of moving to the country or onto a new estate. In the latter case, you are in a different world and need to know how to clear the ground easily – though this also applies to any ruthless garden owner who is brave enough to clear out the previous owners' efforts. After all, if a weed is a plant in the wrong place, a garden full of plants you don't actually want is full of plants in the wrong place – ergo weeds.

The trick here is to smother, and the very best smotherer is wood chip. I know it gets sold in bags but that's a bit hopeless unless you're mulching a window box. Seek out those people who work with wood and who may have chippings (or bark – inferior but definitely usable) to dispose of i.e. carpenters, tree surgeons, fencing merchants and sources of wood chip fuel (they call it fuel and use it as fuel; you call it mulch and mulch with it). Failing wood chip, leaves will also do it if you can get them. Manure is possible but not ideal, nor is straw, unless you know absolutely that they are clear of herbicides, weeds, antibiotics and other random nasties. To clear an area you need to mow or strim the existing greenery down to the ground to start with, then pile on the wood chip 15 to 20 cm (6–8 in) deep. Stand back and admire your work. Weedkill anything daring to stick its head up (though weeds will actually also pull up easier when in a good mulch). Plant through the mulch after you've left it long enough for the greenery underneath to have decomposed a bit.

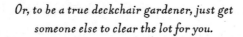

DECKCHAIR WISDOM

Taking over someone else's garden requires you to be ruthless. If it's a very big garden, you could be ruthless in small doses.

Or, to be a true deckchair gardener, just get someone else to clear the lot for you.

FINE GARDENING

All right, thinking caps on: time for Garden University Challenge. No cheating on Google – what do the following mean? Floricanes, haulms, slips, bipinnate, cladode, epiphyte, monoecious, scion, stolon, umbel?

If you know, I suggest you give up on this book. It is not for you. These are terms used in fine gardening, and fine gardening is not for the likes of us. It is, of course, the equivalent of fine dining and is best experienced outside of your home. Just as you are not likely to use a recipe from *MasterChef* for the kids' tea, so you are unlikely to employ fine gardening in your own backyard.

But it's out there, scaring us. When someone is described as a great gardener, this means someone who uses terms such as these and does things like grafting. Do not be intimidated. It is perfectly possible to have apples to cobble dogs with (one of my father's favourite expressions, meaning you have loads and loads of the blessed things) without knowing about pruning, thinning, grease bands (no, not a version of the ubiquitous boy band) or bitter pit. It may be heresy to say so, but the sheer overwhelming number of apples that one totally neglected tree can produce is a nightmare to anyone driven to try to find positive uses for every one of them. Especially since your equally neglectful neighbours will no doubt be trying to get rid of theirs at the same time.

Deckchair gardener, know thyself

It is pretty in a sweet, old-fashioned way to train a fruit tree to a garden wall, if you are fortunate enough to have a garden wall. Espaliers and fans are excellent, but they are as much use to the improper gardener as learning to fly. Smile and move on. Such enterprise is reason enough to look with deep suspicion upon horticultural training, often assumed to be a merit in a professional gardener. I know it sounds daft, but if you, the deckchair gardener, are lucky enough to be able to afford some help in the garden you are unlikely to want someone chafing at the bit in their eagerness to do scarifying and grafting when all you want is for them to shift a pile of gravel. You do not need the expensively trained chef; you need the garden equivalent of the housewife. Someone practical, fast-working and tough. And intelligent. The ability to think things through, anticipate problems and be creative with solutions is more important than knowing what depth to plant a bulb at. (Incidentally, bulbs are actually very good at making their own way to the right depth.)

You need, as an *improper* gardener, to develop a nose for fine gardening. You will find it all over the place: in gardening magazines, books, RHS gardens and the like, and you need to see it coming in order not to be intimidated. The people who go on about it have a living to make and there's lots of mileage in describing and demonstrating obscure garden techniques. It's prestigious and comes with certificates – but you can get along very nicely without it. You are going to be the dreadful gardener who sees a plant ailing and goes out with a spade to dig it up and dump it. That may seem extravagant but do you really have the resources of time and money to coddle it back into feeble, unhappy life? No. Chuck it.

DECKCHAIR WISDOM

Fine gardening is not for us. If you like it, visit gardens of posh houses, the Royal Horticultural Society and the National Trust.

You'll be able to have tea and lemon drizzle cake too if you do.

There is snobbery in gardening as in all other human endeavour, so beware of it and be brave. Cultivate your crap detector before your rose pillar. If you do find yourself falling desperately in love with some obscure plant that will be a nightmare to grow, or stubbornly dream about the joy of plucking a peach from your very own tree, then take every lesson from this book doubly seriously. Make all of your other gardening easier and easier until you have the time and energy left over to pursue your precious pet project, guilt-free and properly. No one is saying you must never fastidiously pin a climbing rose to your house wall on a frame that can be removed when you need to repaint the wall, or spend happy hours doing winter pruning, summer pruning and hard pruning of a carefully trained wisteria. But if you do have such an ambition you will need to give yourself vast quantities of leisure to do it in and must abandon edging the lawn.

You will certainly have come across the relentless garden bullying that usually follows garden advice on television and in magazines. There is never any peace: it's all do this, do that . . . Well, this is my version – what *not* to do.

What not to do in your garden in spring

'The flowers that bloom in the spring,

Tra la,

Breathe promise of merry sunshine —

As we merrily dance and we sing,

Tra la,

We welcome the hope that they bring,

Tra la,

Of a summer of roses and wine,

– and no weeding'

(*The Mikado* . . . apart from the last line)

Plant lilies.

The lily beetle – the red menace that is pretty to look at but horrible to deal with – is far too common now to bother with planting lilies, unless you wish to devote your life to them and their protection (i.e. beetle squishing – not pleasant). Besides, supermarkets sell lilies, totally free of lily beetle poo (don't ask). Though watch that pollen – it stains.

Rake the lawn with a springy wire rake.

Well, I never have. Unless the lawn is your pride and joy, and caring for it is all you ever do, leave the lawn rake in the shed. I believe it is also intended to scrape up all the dead grass and thatch. I wonder what my lawn would look like if I did do it . . . I strongly suspect there might be no grass left.

Aerate the lawn with an aerating implement (or by sticking a garden fork in all over it).

Or not – again, I never have. It's interesting to note that you get given more than one reason for doing it, which is always suspicious. It suggests to me a degree of uncertainty, which someone is trying to disguise by providing plenty of possibilities in case you notice that one of them is utter nonsense. Aerating apparently allows air, water and nutrients to penetrate to the grass roots. Another reason for it is to alleviate soil compaction, but what on earth could you have been doing to squash your lawn so? Anyway, apparently you've flattened it and now it can't breathe.

Well, I thought worms were supposed to do all that aerating and moving stuff into the soil for you. What else are we paying them for? It is also suggested that aerating the lawn lets the stale carbon dioxide out and lets the good oxygen in. But since that carbon dioxide will create climate change, best leave it stuck under the grass, don't we think?

But then there's yet *another* reason offered – and if you believe this one it means you should also be doing the job in the autumn, as aerating allegedly *increases the soil temperature*. I have no idea why you'd want to, but there you go, someone says it does and thinks it's a good thing. And beware of frost, as this can make the lawn heave!

Some people, I believe, follow this exercise by putting stuff like compost down the holes they've made. That means obtaining, spreading and brushing the compost in. But then what if the oxygen can't get in because you laboriously plugged up the holes you've just made like that? Just don't bother – it will only make you irate.

Level the lawn.

This is possibly worth doing if you want to play croquet. Moles and general carelessness on the part of whoever planted your lawn can lead to lumps and hollows. If they don't actually trip you up and you can create the vague impression of a flat surface using your lawnmower, I should leave well alone. If you really can't put up with them, fill your hollows slowly by finding some spare soil (sorry, I can't find any for you – some John Innes compost would do though) and sprinkle it in the hollows up to the top of the neighbouring grass. Stamp it in well and then let the grass accommodate the change and find its new level. Then repeat until it's finally flat.

Humps are harder to deal with. You need to make slits in the turf in an H shape so you can roll the turf back and remove soil from underneath until the turf lies flat when you roll it back. This is much easier for me to write than for you to do.

After learning about having to go to all this effort, you'll probably decide you don't want to play croquet after all. The equipment is very expensive and I understand it can be a very aggressive game. Really best avoided on all counts.

DECKCHAIR WISDOM

Don't take a spirit level to your grass.

Do sit around on your lawn reading and watching the clouds sail by.

Prune roses.

Don't grow roses.

Well, if you are truly dedicated to easy gardening, the most you'll do is grow the odd rambler up a tree and ignore it until it flowers, when you will go and admire it every day. One is supposed to plant a rose outside of the rain shadow of a tree – i.e. a long way away from the trunk – and then train it along a rope or stake into the tree. This is harder than it sounds – a healthy rambler will have lots of shoots and will not take kindly to being fastened to a stake or a

DUNPRUNIN'

37

rope. And you'll fall over it as you wander thoughtfully around the garden after a couple of Pimms.

I have twice planted a rambler along with a very small self-sown sapling and encouraged them to grow up all friendly like, together. This involves now and then taking a rake or similarly long tool and using it to persuade the roses' long, waving and rather prickly stems over a convenient branch of the tree. Oddly, I enjoy this activity. If you can't imagine doing this, best admire other people's roses and leave them all alone. Almost all roses are far too much trouble for the return they give.

Check all houseplants.

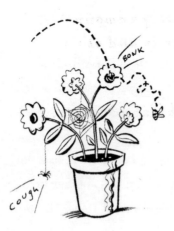

This is to see if they are pot bound (i.e. have grown too big for their pots), starving or dirty (wash them – seriously?) Now, do idle gardeners really have pot plants? What are cut flowers for? Consider trying some silk flowers –

they cheer things up a treat as long as you avoid 'foliage' (they seem able to make very convincing flowers but much less convincing foliage). Otherwise, you could invest in some plastic house plants. You'd still have to dust them occasionally, though. Hey, nothing's perfect.

Put up greenhouse shade netting if the sun is out and conditions are hot.

You'll be lucky – sun? Well, the joys of not having a greenhouse, eh?

Hang yellow sticky traps among plants to catch whitefly and other flying pests ...

... And catch your hair in as you bend down to ...

Check plants regularly for signs of pests.

Sigh.

Trim leggy rosemary bushes to promote bushy new growth.

Don't we also get told not to trim evergreens (which, of course, rosemary is) during frost for fear of promoting new sappy growth that will then get frosted? Not that I'm convinced about that one either.

Sow lettuce from now every two weeks to keep your harvest coming.

Charles Dowding, the organic vegetable expert who really does experiment to find out what works (or doesn't), says no. If you only pick the outside leaves you can go on picking weekly and the lettuce will go on growing for about twelve weeks. But pick, don't cut, if you really must grow lettuce.

Sow hardy annuals directly onto flowerbeds.

Do people really keep little spaces bare in the borders to organize a little banquet for the birds in this way? Nasturtiums maybe. That's it.

DECKCHAIR WISDOM

Don't faff around outside when it still feels like winter.

Do read a good book by the fire, periodically admiring your newly dusted plastic plant.

Feed roses with a proprietary or soluble rose feed.

Nope – no extra feeding unless a soil test tells you that you need to.

Stake plants while the new growth of perennials is still short.

There is no look quite so dated in a garden – except maybe dwarf conifers with heather arranged round a little wishing well set in crazy paving – as staked plants. As our gardens get more relaxed and at ease with themselves, strapping plants to canes or peasticks looks more and more odd. You don't *need* to grow naturally lanky plants like delphiniums or lupins – if you want to save effort, just don't do it.

The trick here is to give up growing things with a natural 'topple' factor. That is, all tall, lanky things like delphiniums, or things with heavy flowers, like dahlias. (I don't know, since I certainly don't stake and grow short dahlias in pots.) I like to grow cardoons in quantity for their long-lasting good looks, from their dramatic cut leaves right up to their bee-enticing flowers. But the flowers are very top heavy – you could cut one and keep it by the door as a handy burglar bop. Mostly, they stand up all by themselves but just sometimes they need a stout stake. (Proving that nothing I say can be totally trusted. Well, you knew that.) And anyway, at home we let ours fall over and then just cut them off.

However, generally all your 'not feeding' pays off as it's the lush, overfed, rather spoiled plants that keel over in the first (inevitable) gale. Treat them tough and they'll usually stay up.

If you live where it's horribly windy, it might help to plant dubiously self-supporting plants where they can lean against a wall, fence or hedge. Reinforce this by planting generously – you don't want spaces between your plants unless you're doing something particular, like growing things in gravel – which will make them tougher anyway. If plants are planted close together they can lean on one another, just like we do when we're weary and wind-blown.

It's important here to think wind breaks – that's fences and hedges rather than walls, as walls can create turbulence when wind belts over them, surprising that poor plant that thought it was safely tucked away. If all else fails and it has fallen over, chop it off. It's very likely it will then regrow to a height and robustness that will stand up. And next year, do a pre-emptive chop before it falls over.

Oh, time for a quick touch of honesty here: plants at path edges can fall over for lack of support at the path edge. Railings help, but I'm afraid you'd have to actually make them. (But they can look really cool, emphasizing the pattern of the path, preventing your own falling-over tendencies and discouraging your paths from unsightly wiggles.) Alternatively, don't plant anything with a falling tendency at the path edge.

DECKCHAIR TIP

Stakes are for vampires. If your plant leans, chop it down and make it try again.

Do grow grasses where it's windy – they stay up and their graceful movement in the wind is a delight.

Hoe weed seedlings.

If you have weed seedlings you haven't been mulching. Well, that's almost true. Cleavers – *Galium aparine*, or: clivers, goosegrass, kisses, stickyweed, stickybud, sticky willy, grip grass, robin-run-the-hedge, velcro weed (this is not a list of many weeds; it's the variety of names for just the one. Kind of made an impact, hasn't it?) – will still make an appearance, defiantly beating any mulch into sad failure. Answer: keep geese – they like eating it (hence 'goosegrass'). The other common names tell you most of what you need to know, except how on earth does it germinate where nothing else does? And is it easy to keep geese?

The main rule is, do not hoe it. The hoe is the instrument of the devil: it leaves disturbed bare soil around emerging plants, which not only looks ugly but brings up more weed seeds. Think *smother* instead – add more mulch. Throw the hoe.

Deadhead daffodils and give them a liquid feed or a sprinkling of bonemeal.

I have rarely deadheaded a daffodil and yet mine always seem perfectly happy to pop up and flower every year. They can look a little miserable as they go over though, so if they are too in-your-face you might want to chop the miserable dead flower bit off. (Leave the leaves though; they need them for six weeks after flowering. Then you can chop them down too.) I had a friend with a field absolutely full of wild daffodils and you may guess that she certainly didn't go around deadheading them every year. Nor feeding them. How do people who make these recommendations imagine wild daffodils manage to thrive? Did none of them read their Wordsworth when they were at school? Did they imagine the poet and his sister were out sprinkling bonemeal as they went?

Bonemeal and chicken manure are sources of phosphorus, which in excess will turn the leaves of your plants yellow, possibly causing you to add some more in a panic, thinking they are starving. Do remember that plants can't just throw up like you can if they are fed too much, so treat them with care. Too much bonemeal is also bad for their roots and, like nitrogen, can get into water courses where there has been too much in the soil. This is not good for our rivers and streams.

I believe that the terrible old habit of tying up daffodil leaves when they've finished flowering has ceased now? But one practice that is just as ugly is planting bulbs in clumps and mowing round them. Be brave and hold on the mowing until the requisite six weeks after the flowering has stopped. Less mowing, and you can spread the bulbs in a pleasant random manner and leave them to seed and spread. But they won't seed if you chop their heads off, will they?

Make new borders by removing turf and digging the soil over. Use a hosepipe to create the new shape of the edges.

No, no, no – no digging, please! Turf will die and then also benefit the soil if you mulch thickly – maybe 15 to 20 cm (6–8 in) for a killing mulch – over the top of whatever you wish to see the back of. And no wiggly hosepipe borders either. We don't have to have ugly gardens just because we're lazy. Come to think of it – why are we making new borders anyway? We probably have more than enough to deal with as it is.

Thin seedlings.

This is not about weedy seedlings, this is about all the flower and vegetable seeds you may have sown in a fit of misguided enthusiasm. The least you can do if you must sow seeds is save yourself the annoying job of thinning them later on by initially sowing very thinly. It is possible. You can pick up the tiniest seed with a sharp pencil that you've licked. (Yes, you can lick a pencil without dying – that's not real lead, you know.) Just lick, pick up seed with pointy bit, carefully place where you want it and the touch of the compost in the seed tray should dislodge it from the pencil. Simples. Well, not if they are great big ones – in which case, use tweezers.

Keep watering these seedlings.

Well, not as often as you think. Wait until they are really dry – most things will tolerate more dry than you think they will. And neither do you need to faff about trying to water from the bottom and watching the compost in the seed tray start floating. Nor do you need to turn the rose on your watering can upside down. Charles Dowding reckons a good direct shower from a pointing-down rose will help toughen them up. Go on – show them who's boss.

Encourage hedgehogs, frogs, toads and thrushes so that they come and eat your slugs and snails.

'Encourage' is one of those garden media words that plague us rather like the slugs and snails. Think also 'lovely', 'interesting' 'inspiring' … But 'encourage' always gives me the giggles: it conjures up a picture of a gardener out there making persuasive little chirruping noises to try and conjure up some useful birds and beasties, in the same sort of way that some strange people irritate cats by making silly noises.

Sad to say, even if encouraged by the many chirps, these obliging creatures are hardly likely to make any significant impact on the mollusc population – they just

give you more wildlife to worry about. And worry you must. For example, never leave a bucket outside right way up all winter. It will get water in it – and maybe even drowned mice, which smell revolting. (No idea how they get in – are they flying mice? But get in they do.) And on occasion, you may find a toad in there and wonder how it plans to get out. (It can't.) Less wildlife, less worry.

DECKCHAIR WISDOM

Do avoid chirruping to your frogs.

Try kissing them – we could all use a prince in our lives.

Fill gaps in flowerbeds with bedding plants.

I have no idea how you come to have gaps in your borders, or how you know about it for sure at this time of year when things are still (we hope) emerging – maybe one of your plants has died. The idea of sticking in some bedding plants to replace it is nightmarish though – in any decent perennial bed they are likely to stick out like a slap on the face. Bedding plants tend to come in rather brave mixed colours and be squat and over floriferous. They look great in pots if you can unmix the colours. But not so much among your perennials.

Start chitting early potatoes: stand them on end in a module tray or egg box and place in a bright, cool, frost-free place.

'Chitting' is getting potatoes to sprout. Have you ever tried stopping the potatoes in your kitchen from sprouting? They are desperate to sprout, whatever you do. If you turn your back for five minutes they will have long stems sticking out all over the place, making you look a right poor housekeeper. If you have the misfortune to have potatoes find their evil way into your compost heap, you will find potato foliage sticking out everywhere come summer. You will never get rid of them without clearing out the whole heap and starting again. By which time you may find if you've used the compost

carelessly that you have potatoes in places you never imagined a spud. So why are you supposed, if you want to grow them in the ground, to cosset them in egg boxes and 'module trays' (whatever they are – I have no idea; I bet you have to pay money for them)?

DECKCHAIR TIP

If you want to grow potatoes, my best recommendation is to throw them away.

Plant your chitted potatoes.

Well, not having chitted them to begin with (see above), we are now spared the backbreaking job of planting them. And also spared the anxiety – how do you place the soil on top of chitted potatoes in a trench without knocking off the stems you've carefully created? Buy fresh ones from the local Farmers' Market.

Lift and divide congested perennials.

This is standard advice regarding clump-forming perennials that I have never followed unless I was looking for some new plants. They are supposed to get impoverished and less productive in their middle if just left. I haven't noticed this. Perhaps this happens if you don't mulch or have a different sort of soil to mine. Anyway, if you have problems in your middles you now know what to do. Dig it up and cut it into bits and replant one of the bits. Find somewhere good (and empty) for the remaining bits. Some people think you should do this in autumn, but you're more likely to want to do this sort of thing in spring when the sun comes out than in autumn when you've had more than enough of the garden. And in my part of the world, where the winters are wet, your replants might well rot if you did them in the autumn.

It's a lot easier, if you want new plants, to just split a piece off the outer edge. But don't try this with a plant that has a pointy root, known as tap root, as you'll likely get no root and a sad bit of plant left wondering why you started chopping at it when it had done you no harm at all.

Use two forks back to back to split your plants.

I wouldn't recommend this rather odd approach if you do decide to dig up your plant in order to split it and get more of them, or in an attempt to deal with its inadequate middle. Hostas have actually been propagated by digging up and splitting in my garden by the tougher among us. But there are very few uses for a garden fork in a garden where you don't play at titillating the soil and all that sort of faffing about, so why on earth you would posses two, I cannot imagine. Neither can most of us balance a plant on its soil ball, and simultaneously shove two forks in: our arms aren't long enough and the plant usually won't sit still while you try.

Better by far to get yourself an old saw that has lost its wood-cutting edge and saw the plant into smaller pieces. With a smaller plant, a breadknife will do – and, indeed, is an invaluable garden tool. In fact, you should never bring home a plant in a pot without then sawing it in half with your breadknife, in order to have two where you once had one. Do that twice and you've paid for the breadknife.

DECKCHAIR TIP

Beware the tap-rooted plants. This does not mean you can turn it on and get hot water. If in doubt, look the plant up before you saw or split.

Do kill off and replace plants with temperamental middles. Just get something new.

Plant summer-flowering bulbs such as gladioli by the end of May, and make sure they have a well-drained position in full sun.

Dame Edna would be proud of you.

Harden plants off.

This refers to the tender plants that have come straight out of a cosy, warm polytunnel or greenhouse and now need to face the outside world. The idea is that you introduce them to the cruel, cold world gradually, a bit like the way you paddle into the sea when you visit the east coast for a swim at this time of year.

In theory, you move your delicate plants from a heated greenhouse to a cool one, or maybe bring all your seedling trays out during the day and take them back in at night. Then, after a while, you put everything in a cold frame. You open the cold frame during the day and close it at night, gradually increasing the time it's open for, until boom! Full exposure!

Except that the weather is not like the sea. It doesn't just get gradually colder, it gets hot, cold and in-between, until you don't know whether your plants should be in or out and when, or whether the cold frame should be open, closed or something in the middle – and then you will have an unexpected hard frost that kills the lot stone dead.

I've never been able to get to grips with all this myself, and think that if you don't grow veggies it's quite easy to ignore the whole incomprehensible business. If you are going to worry about it, I suppose the answer is simply not to grow tender plants. Deckchair gardeners won't have a greenhouse or cold frame anyway, unless they've inherited one. Charles Dowding thinks it's nonsense too, and he suggests that you just take your seedlings out of the greenhouse and plant them in the soil (which would definitely keep the roots warmer than leaving them in seed trays or pots). Then if frost threatens, cover them with fleece (that's the kind you buy in your garden centre, not M&S). This applies equally well to tender ornamentals and even those cheerful bedding plants you've just bought at the local garden centre far too early. Just chuck fleece over and weigh it down with a handy stone.

I have spent many minutes wandering round the garden in a hopeless search for a handy, preferably clean, stone for such purposes. It probably helps that frosty nights are not usually windy nights, so maybe you can abandon the rather fruitless search for stones. But you do keep a lot of fleece handy, I hope? If not – now's the time to start.

Plant early flowers where they won't get the morning sun (to protect against frost).

The idea here is that flowers that get frosted and then shone on by happy spring sunshine will scorch. So you are supposed to plant them where they will miss the early morning sun, or you must rush out at midnight and cover them up.

As if.

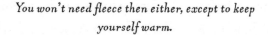

DECKCHAIR TIP

Avoid all tender plants that may need to wander around in and out of greenhouses and cold frames.

You won't need fleece then either, except to keep yourself warm.

Continue pruning ...

Well, you have been at it non-stop, I hope? Haven't you? Day and night?

Do the Chelsea Chop.

Sounds like a dance from the 1960s, doesn't it? It's a good name – which is why we need to be a little cautious of it. You wouldn't want to be promoting a new way of caring for your garden called the May Massacre, would you? Though you could just as well call the Chelsea Chop that: it does involve cutting down plants just as they are just beginning to show that they are going to flower their little socks off for you. How kind is that?

Well, there may be some things which benefit from a hack back in late May but I haven't been in the habit of it myself, except things that were also hanging over the paths. I wonder if this was a technique that arose when there were less late-flowering plants to be bought in our garden centres and nurseries? There's still a tendency to regard June as the garden month, but that is a terribly dated idea. There are good flowering plants which will keep your garden going now until September and October and all of the time in between. So you might gain most not by Chelsea Chopping but by visiting gardens, nurseries and garden centres religiously every month to discover what can be flowering in every month. And research late-flowering plants online – some of them don't present well in pots, so you won't find them in every garden centre. Spring-flowering plants tend to be short, as they don't have long to grow. But later-flowering plants have all season to get bigger so they often will get lanky and too big to sit in pots in a garden centre.

DECKCHAIR WISDOM

*You can play around with cutting plants down
at this time of year if you really want to.
They'll generally grow back – shorter.*

You can also not bother with any of that.

Sow seeds for the vegetable garden.

I say no to this not only because, in my opinion, spring is
far too late to sow vegetable seeds. It's actually because a
dear friend of mine who was totally exhausted by her day
job was fretting because she hadn't got her seeds sown,
and when I suggested buying plug plants said that it 'feels
like cheating'. This is the kind of madness that people
can succumb to when they garden, and I'm here to warn
you off it. Who are you cheating? The kind people who
make a living growing seeds for you, so that you can
assist them making their living, while they assist you in
not becoming exhausted making *your* living? Take all the
help you can get if you work full-time and still insist on

growing your own fruit and vegetables – you owe it to your friends and relations. They do not like to see you sad and tired, even if it means they can eat a super-fresh bean occasionally.

Visit Chelsea Flower Show.

Well, maybe not, if you take seriously what I'm saying about the times you can have plants flowering these days. Chelsea is unrealistic in the choice of plants people put together in their showy gardens. The designers tend to get their suppliers to slow flowering down or bring flowering on early, as do the nurseries displaying their wares. So it's all out of time, in order to have a big, flowering display for the show at the end of May, which is the cusp between spring and summer.

So if you go and get tempted to make your big plant shopping list at Chelsea, you will end up with a garden with an early display, followed by not so much after June. This effect can be exacerbated by the joy of rushing off to your local nursery or garden centre to buy new plants when the sun first begins to feel warm and spring-like. Best to spread out your buying: don't stop until October.

The best time to buy a plant is when your garden is telling you – i.e. by becoming boring – that you need one. And when you can then see what you're getting, as it's already flowering. A great bonus of late buying is that plants that flower later tend to flower for longer.

DECKCHAIR WISDOM

Do shop for plants throughout the whole growing season.

Going shopping is a great break from the garden.

Specialist gardens 1

GENERAL PRINCIPLES

The British garden of popular imagination is a kind of hotchpotch with everything slightly garden-y thrown in. If you're very unlucky, it will feature concrete Buddhas and gnomes fishing in a plastic pond. Latterly, it has only got worse and worse.

Once upon a time, you might have had a lawn, various different kinds of 'essential' plants, shrubs, dahlias, vegetables, trees, compost heaps, water features, gnomes and many other things I may have forgotten. Nowadays, you may have all that (especially the dahlias) but you will also have gone ecological, so you will have beehives, bug houses, birdfeeders with delectable bird foods like revolting insects, storage for same delectable foods and revolting insects, a water butt or several, stakes, raised beds – and so it goes on and on and on. You must remember that whatever else you may be, if you start gardening you are now a 'market'. This means that many desperate people are spending their working lives trying to invent things for you to buy, and then they are trying to find willing garden writers, broadcasters and – these days – bloggers to tell you how necessary buying these things is.

I tend to assume that an improper gardener is also an impecunious gardener, and I appreciate that may not always be the case. But if it weren't so, lazy gardeners would just get a team of gardeners to do it all for them. You can see that gardening is not only liable to be hard work without that team of gardeners but also very expensive, so it's a good idea while cultivating your garden to also cultivate a rather cynical and suspicious response to the garden world. There are even dreadful things called advertorials. These are adverts dressed up as proper, objective information, and as you can guess, they are nothing of the sort. Be deeply suspicious and watch out for those. I run a website for thinking gardeners (www.thinkingardens.co.uk) and almost daily get invited to accept an article written solely to invite someone to click a link to some seller's website (and yes, I say no to the lot).

So, contemplate all this, look out at your sorry weedy patch and despair. Nothing like a bit of despair to motivate us all – I'm hoping it will motivate you to start making thoughtful choices. You may be wondering whether there's any way you can actually do nothing at all out there, and desperately hoping so.

Consider your options

One option is to get rid of any unhelpful partner you may have acquired, and then take yourself off to your favourite bookshop. Preferably one with a loo and comfortable seats, so you can select an interesting book and browse while you seat yourself near the gardening section and wait for your prey. You are looking for a likely alternative partner who is clearly very interested in gardening books, preferably of a 'how to' variety'. You then strike up a conversation about how interesting gardening might be (let's stay honest here and stay with '*may* be' or '*could* be'). If they demonstrate an enthusiasm for tough garden work, you've hit the spot. The rest is up to you, since this is not a book on how to set up a date, and perhaps you could pass some of your waiting time reading such a useful book, if necessary.

Alternatively, you may be stuck with a beloved partner and fifteen unabandonable small children, in which case the above is not a good ploy. Here, you require advice for truly minimal gardening. Sadly and truthfully, if you have a patch of anything out there you will have to do *something* to it. Even if you pave the lot (which needs planning permission unless you use permeable paving) you will occasionally need to clean it a bit or the paving will by some mysterious means begin to develop weeds, then slippery moss and earth will begin to appear on top of the paving, under which the paving will eventually disappear completely. This is how archaeology happens. Cleaning it now and then manages to just about keep entropy (the universe's preference to move from order to disorder) at bay.

So if you can bear to do a little something out there – when it's not raining, windy or too cold (or hot) – then let's consider what that thing might be. My point here is that you will not be attending to the kind of garden described above, with every possible kind of garden thing you can shove in it. Think about it: every thing of any sort in any garden will at some point require attention. Even if that is to throw it away.

So, no, it will not be a 'full of bits' garden, it will be a specialist garden. And this could be exciting. You may realize, for example, that you could be very happy growing tomatoes in a large greenhouse. Out go the lawn, the weeds, the trees, the shrubs – and everything else. You will just have a delectable metal greenhouse (wood equals maintenance, whereas aluminium enables you to just about get away with cleaning the glass now and then) and a path to and around it. If your garden is a bit too big for a greenhouse covering nearly all of it to be affordable, you may need a partner with a different obsession to you to use up the rest of the space. Sadly, football might not be best, given all that glass to protect, though a nice brick wall might sort that one out.

If you think 'specialist garden', you see, a world of infinite possibilities arises of the things you might actually want to do and – this word is important – *enjoy* doing. The idea being that you decide what you will focus on and get rid of everything else that gets in the way of that and/or demands any unpleasant time or effort. You won't need to stop at that – there may well also be ways in which you can minimize the effort involved in your favoured activity, but you will have instantly cut out an enormous amount of things you don't want to do. So here are some suggestions to get you going.

A specialist garden should either be full of something you love and desperately want in your life (like a particular plant, water, birds and birdfeeders, giant vegetables or a lawn), or it may involve an activity you love (this may be lying down dozing, hedge cutting, deadheading, weeding – people have odd tastes). But the point is that most people dilute the pleasure of the activity or the garden by having too much variety in their gardens and thus lumbering themselves with unwanted tasks. Be ruthless with the things and/or the activity and your garden suddenly becomes a source of pleasure. Honesty warning: this will not happen overnight – it might take some setting up. Worth it though.

So I offer some possibilities and the easiest way to do them. You don't necessarily need to choose just one, but do give up the idea of the common, too full of everything, garden.

DECKCHAIR WISDOM

Creating a totally different kind of garden will be daring and exciting.

You will find a lot of people quite shocked and disapproving. Some of you will enjoy that.

A GRASSES GARDEN

A specialist garden will enable you to do amazing things as you focus on one area, such as ornamental grasses, which are very beautiful. Many grow big and robust, and some will seed madly, so you could very soon fill your garden if you let them. The point is not to have a selection of several kinds of grasses, as they don't set each other off well in a collection, all being rather – grass-like. In fact, just oblige me and *never* plant a variety of grasses together in a border and then ask me to admire it.

Moreover, a collection would demand the hard work of keeping them arranged and separate and treated differently. No – you will just have one sort, one of the best, and revel in it. Personally, I'd recommend a garden full of *Miscanthus* – one of the tough varieties, like *Miscanthus sinensis* 'Undine', for example. They will flower and look beautiful in late summer, then delight you throughout autumn and winter until you reluctantly strim (with a proper blade, not that silly bit of plastic 'string' that is standard issue) them down in spring so they can start all over again fresh. Leave the strimmings where they lie and they will mulch and feed the grass. Job done. When they are still too small to make sufficient mulch for themselves, you will need to mulch with wood chip or bark.

They will be absent, then dull, in spring, since that is when they start their new growth, so you might just think of planting spring bulbs in amongst them – perhaps daffodils followed by camassias. There are several different kinds of these and all are great, so if you feel inclined – experiment.

Other excellent choices for ornamental grasses are varieties of *Molinia caerulea* subsp. *arundinacea*, *Stipa brachytricha* or *Deschampsia cespitosa*. These have the virtue of seeding like mad, so if you can clear the site rather as if you were going to have a lawn, plant as many as you can afford of one of these and keep the spaces weeded for a while (that may be a couple of years), you could end up with a sea of beauty. It can also do this if you don't weed so much but mulch in between (although they can sometimes manage to seed even through a mulch). If you are wise, grow several experimentally before buying a garden full, just to be sure they like you.

If having just one kind of grass seems a trifle dull to you, it's also possible to raise the aesthetic by adding some tough perennials amongst the grasses after your spring bulbs have shot their bolt. I have done this with some of the tough varieties of *Crocosmia*, and can vouch for 'Lucifer'.

As specialist gardens go, one filled with an ornamental grass looks amazing and is wonderfully easy to look after. It is the windy gardener's ideal solution (I'm referring to the weather here, you know). Refer to a book like Roger Grounds' *The Plantfinder's Guide to Ornamental Grasses* or *Gardening with Grasses* by Michael King and Piet Oudolf, and choose your grasses. I put 'grasses' in the plural here because I do think you would be wise to try one or two to see which ones suit you before you indulge yourself in a magical mass of them.

DECKCHAIR TIP

Grasses are one of the few plants with three seasons' appeal, so pick a good one and love it.

Ignore those people, who have not yet quite died out, who deplore the ornamental grasses trend. They are just so last century.

A HEDGE GARDEN

For this one, I'm afraid you will need to do some hedge cutting. Not everyone can hedge cut. It's one of those skills you either have or you don't – the ability to cut in a straight line by eye. Or even a curvy line – it takes the same skill. And strong arms. If you can do this, and you actually enjoy it, this could be for you. If you can't, you may be able to afford to hire someone who can to do it for you (if the garden isn't too big).

The point of hedges in this context is to create pattern and sculptural shape, as well as to cover the ground so entirely that the hedges and narrow paths between them are all you ever need to care for. I'm sure that the real wow factor at the Veddw House Garden is the moment when you arrive and look over the pattern of hedges and columns in the garden below you – a year-round pleasure shock. Humans are designed to see patterns and to respond to them.

For instance, you could try to create a classic maze. For a suitable and thrilling example look for pictures of the laurel maze at Glendurgan Garden in Cornwall – although forget, perhaps, the fun getting-lost element. You probably have no space for that to be realistic and it would have to be a high hedge, which means ladders and effort. But what a maze potentially offers is a visible pattern. Think of sinuous curves or a pattern composed of straight lines and angles. All the better if you have a small garden, as you could pack it with hedges at a reasonable price if you started with bare-rooted plants in winter.

One option is to abandon the idea of walking between the hedges and instead make it look a solid mass, but leaving just enough space to get at the hedges for cutting (if you can find images of the laurels at Rousham Garden you will see the idea). Or vary the pattern by using different hedging plants. This kind of garden will be especially exciting if you have one of those town houses in a terrace where you look out over the garden every morning when you clean your teeth. But if your prime view is from ground level, you will want to work out a pattern that reads in layers of different heights, one hedge playing against another. This is very tricky to do for those of us who find it difficult to plan in three dimensions. Having done it, I'd recommend you create a ground plan and plant your hedge along it. Then as the hedge grows, start cutting it with a helper to tell you where to cut to keep the hedge behind the one you are cutting exposed in a pleasing way. I'd strongly recommend doing your research and getting a proper idea of the possibilities and what you want to achieve before you begin (Veddw – veddw.com – is a good place to start).

Choosing the right hedge

The trouble may be in choosing a hedging plant. Yew is a good option (and no slower than most) if you live somewhere relatively dry. Sadly, it is susceptible to one horrible thing: phytopthora, a fungal disease. Similarly, box has two different fungal diseases. And recently our own beautiful and apparently unperturbable holly has developed holly blight and started shedding its lower branches. This is so upsetting, as the shine on a holly leaf usually makes it look glowing with health. Maybe we should all give up and just decide to grow fungus.

At the moment (fingers crossed) if you garden somewhere with high rainfall and a damp atmosphere your best evergreen bet might be cherry laurel (*Prunus laurocerasus*), which has fat shiny leaves and a plebeian reputation – but see its renowned use at Rousham to disabuse your mind of the lowly connotation. Both beech (*Fagus sylvatica*) and hornbeam (*Carpinus betulus*) keep their coppery leaves through the winter when clipped as hedges, so while not evergreen they have the same kind of impact and could display a dramatic contrast in your design. Beech also comes in two colours – green and a kind of variable purple – so it would be possible to just use beech to get this effect. I have a dual beech hedge that is purple on one side and green on the other and have to periodically (every couple of years or so) push my way down the middle with loppers in hand, to ensure that the two plants are kept separate. It sounds awful, and you do need a hard hat on, but it only takes an hour or so. Instead, you could randomly mix the two for a more abstract effect. Beech and hornbeam have the virtue of

being fast growing – that will be nice at first but later on may mean cutting twice a year.

There are a good many other plants that can be kept as hedges, such as roses, privet, *Lonicera*, hebe, but be careful you don't replace climbing up ladders and reaching up with too much bending down. All these hedges should ideally be the right size for you to cut comfortably while standing on the ground. Leave the clippings as mulch if you dare, to make it all easier – if you have earth paths and start by mulching those with wood or bark chippings you could just let these lie, topping up the gradually decaying chippings as your hedges grow so your clippings begin to replace your chippings.

You may baulk at the idea of this garden, imagining your neighbour's initial response to the absence of flowers, bedding plants and gnomes (until they see the result when they're cleaning their teeth). But think of all the nesting opportunities you will be providing for the birds. No need to buy special twee little birdhouses (we've been warned off several varieties of those anyway, as bad for birds). You can add some seats and sit there reading in peace and quiet with no disturbing garden tasks to do, as long as you've clipped – out of the nesting season. The nesting season, come to think of it, is a great alibi for not clipping when you really can't be bothered.

DECKCHAIR WISDOM

Hedges are the delight of all those who love order and pattern.

Hedge cutting is one of those garden skills that are in great demand, so if you need one you should be able to find a good hedge cutter to help you out.

What not to do
in your garden
in summer

'Summer has set in with its usual severity.'

Samuel Taylor Coleridge

We all know that the living is supposed to be easy. Why on earth would we be gardening, then? Time to get out the deckchair and doze. It's also when most people go on holiday, so do be careful you haven't got anything that will pine away and die when you go.

For large, quality roses remove all secondary buds from the flower stems.

Well, there's a job you never thought of doing before. You can put it on – and then cross it off – your list right now. Ordinary flowers will satisfy us.

Lift the bulbs you have removed from display beds and left to ripen in trenches.

Enough now. Let's not get silly. You don't have 'display' beds, and if you did you'd leave bulbs to ripen happily where they are. Unless they are tulips, in which case you'll be lucky to get any to survive in soil. Treat yourself to some new colours next year.

Sow biennials.

No. Life's far too short.

Deadhead.

Well, this is the task for you if you feel like poncing around the garden with a pair of scissors and a glass in hand singing 'The Flowers that Bloom in the Spring, Tra-la' (see page 32). Sharp scissors are probably better than secateurs because they have finger holes and open and close seamlessly: secateurs have to have their blades released, which is a faff, and they are easier to drop. But otherwise, this is a task best avoided wherever possible. Experts tell us it helps plants to keep producing more flowers but they don't say that when telling us how wonderful rose hips are. I'm not sure it's worth the effort, and many plants really don't seem to need it.

Annuals, which you are hoping will flower their little heads off all summer, might need it, but there are a lot of them that drop their deadheads all by themselves. Research your purchases online and buy ones described as 'self-cleaning'. This does not mean they wash behind their own ears. It generally means the petals will drop off the plant all by themselves when the flower has gone over. There *are* some flowers that shed water readily from their petals and also get referred to as 'self-cleaning', but that is just one of those esoteric horticultural page fillers for when garden editors get desperate for copy. Just when did flowers start getting dirty? It is apparently also said of some plants that they 'bury their dead'. I bet you never imagined they would be out there with a spade digging graves as soon as your back was turned, did you? I understand it means that the new flowers smother the old ones, which, when you come to think of it, sounds just as unpleasant. But if it doesn't involve you deadheading then it has to be good.

Cut laurel hedges with secateurs to stop the leaves getting ragged.

Our garden is surrounded by neighbouring houses, which when we arrived were either perched above us or totally unscreened. The effect when we went out into the garden was rather as a goldfish might feel in one of those old round bowls they used to circulate in. It was not that we went out there to do anything that would excite our neighbours – sadly the British climate doesn't lend itself to that sort of excitement in the garden very often – it's more that knowing I can be seen makes me self-conscious. The pleasant wander in the garden in my nightclothes, so effective for getting my dose of vitamin D, becomes an embarrassment. So I wanted screening, and I wanted it fast.

I contemplated Leyland cypress (*Cupressus x lelandii*), which can grow 13.7 m (15 yd) high in sixteen years, but even this seemed a long time and the trouble is, they don't stop there. They go on and on until your neighbours come round to confront you about it with a sledgehammer.

Then I came across a reference to screening with cherry laurel (*Prunus laurocerasus*) and I had my answer.

It grows fast but it also stops at about 13.7 m high. And it's evergreen, which means pyjamas outdoors in winter if you want. It's also cheap to buy and then seeds itself madly so that you are never without a few babies to give away, which is a mixed blessing. Generally, we've grown them as large shrubs, just pruning them away from the paths – though pruning is a rather swanky word for taking a hedge trimmer and cutting off all the growth that's getting in the way then mowing it up (this is the great advantage of grass paths).

But there are places where I want a close-cut, 'proper' hedge, usually because I planted the laurels too near a path. You are often recommended to cut these with – would you believe – secateurs. This is mad. Because laurel has big, fat leaves the theory is that you mustn't chop up the leaves with a hedge trimmer or they will look unsightly. Reader, I have hedge-trimmered and seen no ill effects. I confess that it was a little while before I went back specifically to check, and it may be that they grow new leaves very fast so the lacerated leaves get lost to sight. There may well have been a dreadful time that I missed because I was looking the other way. If you are concerned about the potential dreadfulness it might be a good idea to plant something terribly interesting and unmissable on the opposite side to the laurel hedge, so that no one ever notices its ugly phase. If it does have one.

Laurel does have a dangerous side: the leaves contain cyanide and benzaldehyde, which chopping or distilling releases. It's fine in the open air – no reported deaths – but that is why it smells of bitter almond.

DECKCHAIR TIP

Use laurel for screening – and start a laurel shop, too, and sell the babies.

Don't inhale.

Prune apple trees.

I'm sure this is an excellent idea, but we have never tried it. We have cut our rangy-looking apple trees back in winter, so as to improve the shape and eliminate some of the branches that were way out of reach. This is not supposed to be why you prune, and there are mysterious differences between summer pruning and winter pruning, which is all the territory of the Fine Gardener. We have far more apples than we manage to keep and eat without any such fancy activity. And I would have thought that if you prune your apple trees in summer, the hard little apples would be likely to bounce painfully off your head as the disturbance makes them fall off. So if you're not careful you *won't* be left with enough for you and the birds.

DECKCHAIR TIP

If you must have a fruit tree, get an apple on dwarf rootstock, so you have a chance of reaching the fruit.

Then try not to fret about it. It'll either fruit or it won't.

Remove rose suckers.

This is a nightmare job and makes me hate whoever it was who sold me some grafted rugosa roses. It is about removing the emerging stems of the plant that your rose was grafted on to, as the plants that roses are grafted on to have a nasty habit of taking over, resulting in you having a wild rose instead of whatever you carefully chose. I believe that my rugosa roses would have been fine on their own roots and that would have saved me ever having to think about the horrendous sucker problem. You can't just go round chopping the wrong shoots off – providing you can tell which is wrong and which is right. No, you must excavate and cut the shoots off underground, as close to the rootstocks as possible. What on earth does that mean? And what do you cut them with? This is a good way to ruin your secateurs.

Sad to say, ours just get the wrong shoots chopped off low down. I recognize these shoots by looking up a picture of them every year to be sure. The rose that gives me the most trouble is a *Rosa rugosa* 'Blanche Double de Coubert', which as well as being a bit unpronounceable (especially if you don't want to sound pretentious) spoils in the rain. If we're ever having a dry summer, you can bet your life these roses will come out, and I'll have a sniff and forgive them everything for their wonderful scent and beautiful white flowers. And then it will rain and the flowers turn to mush. A real drought-buster, this plant.

Truly, it is best to ask your supplier to sell you only roses grown on their own roots.

Water.

I'd like to claim that if you mulch you won't need to water anything in a drought apart from those things you've just recently planted. Well, that may be true for us in the wet west of the British Isles, but it seems that whenever we venture to the east of the country in high summer we find ourselves horrified by the dismal dried-up look of the gardens. Which may also be in the grip of a hosepipe ban.

Best advice? Go west, where it's mostly wet. Or make sure you plant things that grow well in dry soil. There are several books simply on that subject alone.

Do everything – and do it fast.

If you read the relentless messages like this about what you are supposed to be doing out there, you will begin to wonder if a garden is really worth having. If you're not careful, pleasures will dissolve into burdensome tasks that reprimand you as soon as you stick your nose out of the door. You will not dare read a gardening magazine or newspaper with a gardening column for fear you will discover some dreadful oversight on your part. Some of our visitors go out of their way to tell us how much they have appreciated all the seats that we have as they have gone round the garden, and some tell us they never sit in their own garden. Well, I don't want to turn a pleasure into a chore, but I do think this is the time of year when you should be getting out and enjoying it all. And if you can't – take a picnic to the local park.

DECKCHAIR WISDOM

Don't read the garden press or watch gardening programmes on television – you'll never sleep.

Do learn to relish your bit of outside, whatever it looks like.

Specialist Gardens 2

A LAWN GARDEN

The specialist garden comes in many varieties from labour saving to hard work – but it has to be hard work you love, remember. A lawn garden is an easy option, though you can make it difficult if you fancy, or make it more difficult over time. You could choose to have one big lawn: just a big expanse of rough or manicured grass, depending on your preference. Sounds just too boring to bear? Well, a one-off effort of planting bulbs in the lawn in the autumn would give you some spring pleasure – and a good excuse not to go near said lawn until six weeks after the last bulb goes over. But it will look scruffy while you wait in desperate anticipation to get in there with the mower. You might do better just to be soothing and stick to plain grass.

Add a tree ...

Still a bit bored? Add a tree. A solitary tree, elegantly placed towards one corner. It could be an apple tree, if you fancy picking the fruit and don't mind mowing the windfalls. Ignore all cultural advice regarding fruit tree care, but make sure to cut your apple in half before you bite it. This makes sure it doesn't have anything wriggly inside it, or that if it does, you discover it with your eyes instead of your tongue. Be prepared to let the birds and wasps have a good share – there should still be plenty for you.

If that sounds like too much trouble, you need an ornamental tree – which must not be a winter-flowering cherry (*Prunus x subhirtella 'Autumnalis'*)! Sounds great, doesn't it, a winter-flowering cherry? A tree that will cheer you up with beautiful flowers in the middle of winter. But it's not quite like that: it doesn't flower as generously as the spring cherries; it's rather sparse; the flowers are somewhat little – and worse, it mostly flowers against a dull, grey winter sky, which manages to render the flowers invisible. And cherries have a notoriously short life, so you will be faced with disposing of it at some point if you hang around, putting up with it.

So what could it be? An *Amelanchier canadensis* would be a good choice. It will give you pretty white flowers in spring, when there is more chance of a blue sky to set them off, and it will add beautiful bronzy leaves before the flowers are quite done. Then in autumn it will go flaming red for several weeks. Worried about leaf drop? Just mow them up. It is quite small, with a tendency to become a bush, and the delicacy of the leaves will not provide screening should that be your cunning plan.

You may prefer the ubiquitous magnolia. It is ubiquitous because it really performs and makes our cities a spring delight. The *stellata* variety is excellent, named after the 'star' effect of its petals, which means it's not one of the tulip-shaped, thick-petalled wonders, which are also beautiful and classy. You will doubtless be bewildered by names and possibilities, so contact a specialist nursery, either online or in the flesh, and consult. Or ask someone who has one you find especially delectable.

Other goodies from my own experience would be the *Sorbus*. The one I know well, as I have two, is *hupehensis*, a recommendation I picked up from Robin Lane Fox in the beginner gardener's bible *Better Gardening*. It is a manageable size with a grey-green leaf, and ours has white berries. Don't believe the tale that birds will shun white berries. Sometimes they do and sometimes they don't. But there is a quiet pleasure in watching the blackbirds happily feeding.

Go for the shaggy look

Beneath these satisfying pleasures is your lawn. You will need to mow it, at least after the bulb hiatus. If you dread the noise and machinery, you'll be pleased to hear that push mowers have been revived. They enable you to cut your (small) lawn without making your neighbours hate you, and give you the best excuse not to go to a gym. Leave the cuttings *in situ* as mulch and your job is done. Cut it high and not very often – the slightly shaggy look has happily come into fashion (as you will certainly be telling those slightly critical neighbours who are peering over your fence).

However, you might be a potential lawn fanatic and may choose to do all those mad lawn things besides mowing now and then. You know: scarifying, feeding, sticking garden forks in it, weeding, rolling and all that stuff. But do all this only if it will give you enormous pleasure, both in the doing and in contemplating the results. Stripes are some people's dream; some people make patterns with the stripy effect on a perfect lawn – circles, spirals, that kind of thing. There's happiness for you.

DECKCHAIR WISDOM

Lawns can go either way. A once-a-week mow in the summer, or a lifetime of total dedication to perfection. Prepare yourself!

A MEADOW GARDEN

Don't even think about the currently popular idea of a meadow, which is a field full of bright annuals in primary colours, like a hanging basket gone rampant. That is an imitation of an arable field before modern weedkillers deprived us of all those flowers, and, of course, it has the arable bit removed. It can look quite amazing but you can't have one – they are too much work. It is not easy to grow weeds on purpose and you have to start afresh every year. What's more, it helps to have a plough and something to do the seeding for you (this is called agriculture). What's even more, you have to hope that boring, coarse perennial weeds don't get in there and ruin the effect. Or you will have to weed them out to keep it pretty. When people say meadows are hard work, this is what they are thinking of. However a miniature version of the traditional hay meadow is not so bad. You may certainly be able to have a meadow that's relatively easy to maintain if you have this kind that's modelled on a hay meadow and not (as above) an arable field. See below.

There's rough and 'rough'

If you are fortunate enough to acquire a rough field you should take the following approach seriously, and if you have a patch of rough grass the same applies. A patch of rough lawn might be a fair start, but 'rough' is the operative word. If it has previously been cared for by someone who weedkilled, aerated, fertilized and generally faffed about with it, it will be ruined for your purposes. Your ideal is grassland that still retains the seeds and plants of the traditional meadow. Don't be discouraged if what you have is growing nettles and coarse grasses and generally looks a mess. If you keep mowing and removing the grass for long enough you will get finer and better grasses, and you will open up the possibility of the return of the wildflowers you long to see. It will take several years, and you will need to have somewhere to dispose of the mowings (conventionally known as 'hay'). Hay makes a great mulch for fruit trees, so you may consider having an orchard next to your meadow.

Typically on the larger size, a meadow could also be very sweet in miniature. You can fill it full of bulbs for spring if you are prepared to get in there with a bulb planter and some enthusiasm at least once. You can get a supply of bulbs from somewhere like Peter Nyssen, who sell in large quantities at reasonable prices. Spring will be a delight thereafter, provided squirrels, rabbits or moles don't spoil your plans (in which case you need my

previous book *Outwitting Squirrels: And Other Garden Pests and Nuisances).*

Then simply let it all grow until the end of June, and sometime after that, mow. Or strim. If your meadow's very full of coarse grass, nettles, docks and similarly depressing stuff that a mower can't cope with, you may have to strim and rake off the result, and that is hardly easy gardening, unless you can persuade someone else to do it for you. The alternative is to hold on the bulbs for a few years and mow earlier and more frequently – always removing the cuttings. Your purpose is to discourage and ultimately lose the coarse stuff, which repeated cutting and removing the cuttings will do. When you have arrived at that point, *then* plant the bulbs and mow after the end of June. As the meadow improves year on year, your work will get less and your pleasure greater. If you are able to mow and remove at the end of June your life will be easy. You may like to add an extra mow in September or October just to tidy it up for the winter, when you will be looking at low grass for two or three months.

It also helps to add seeds of yellow rattle (*Rhinanthus minor*), which is parasitic on grass and helps the reducing coarseness regime as well as looking pretty in flower. Scrape the ground a bit and scatter the seeds in late summer.

Is that a meadow or a field?

If you have a proper field you may be able to persuade a local farmer to mow and take the hay if you're lucky. If you find you don't get the wildflowers you long for, you can buy plants and plant them into your meadow, and if they are the right plants for the place (consider wetness, dryness, weather and what traditionally grew in your locality, if possible) they will seed for you. The caution about doing that with any large meadow is that it may have varieties of plants that have specialized in your area, with minute but important differences from those in the next county. That is an ecological difference worth preserving if possible. One way to preserve the particularity of your local plants is to ask for some of the hay from a neighbouring meadow, if you have such a thing, and scatter that around in your meadow after cutting, for the seed. If you begin to take all this seriously and enthusiastically then look online and you may find local meadows, local meadow conservation societies and even a national meadows day. And thereby, lots of help.

One thought: it's often suggested that you can turn your lawn into a meadow, and this is true. But you will be giving up the sitting-out space that the lawn may have been offering. A meadow is only suitable for sitting on in winter, when it's low cut, and sitting out in snow and pouring rain isn't most people's greatest ambition.

DECKCHAIR TIP

Meadows have become frantically fashionable, but these are the ones in primary colours made of annuals, sown and tended annually.

You will need to virtue signal to keep your end up with people who assume this is what you mean when you mention your meadow garden. The words you will need are ones like 'ecological', 'wildlife friendly', 'conservation', 'butterflies' and 'bees'.

A GRAVEL GARDEN

People often complain about being inflicted with a heavy clay soil. In my experience a mulch of bark or wood chippings will sort that if you give it time. But Derry Watkins of Special Plants, a nursery that grows and sells unusual plants from all over the world (http://www.specialplants.net/), has an alternative approach: bury your garden in gravel. Having seen the results this seemed to be a great way forward for those who want to garden in the most unbelievably easy way, so I interviewed Derry to find out all about it.

And, yes, she did start with heavy clay, on a Cotswold hillside. Derry had read of a 1950s alpine grower experimenting with the best medium for growing his plants. He discovered that to grow alpines the best proportion of gravel to soil was just 10 per cent soil: practically nothing but 'dirty gravel'. Derry then met John d'Arcy who was growing his South African plants in 10 cm (4 in) of

gravel on top of his good garden soil. Encouraged by this information Derry scraped off the topsoil to use elsewhere in the garden (I think you might possibly skip that bit if your soil isn't very good, but read on), weedkilled all the perennial weeds and then stuck 20 cm (8 in) of gravel on the top of the exposed subsoil. She then added plants straight out of their pots, with the compost still attached, into the gravel.

Importantly, this was clean gravel. Use gravel sized half a centimetre to two-and-a-half centimetres (a quarter of an inch to one inch). The exact size may not be very critical but Derry has found that it's important that the sizes are variable, as that creates a more stable surface for walking on. And, yes – this was on clay soil, with no shortage of rain, and yet you can walk among your plants.

Treat 'em mean ...

This is not a system for any old plants though. The ones that love it and look right are either Mediterranean in origin or alpine. The Mediterranean plants are characterized by being sun loving, not needing or wanting too much moisture and can be borderline hardy. Both Derry and I are convinced that in the west of the country more plants are lost in winter to rot rather than cold – Derry found that where she added some good soil underneath the gravel the plants would grow away like mad and then die in the winter. These are plants that do better the hungrier they are. Those of you who are paying attention may note that once again we discover that the importance of feeding plants is vastly exaggerated and should be taken with a pinch of salt (the advice, not the plant food). Derry has, apart from that regretted experiment with adding soil, never fed any of the plants in her gravel beds. She points out that plants make their own food from light and water. (It's called photosynthesis, and you learned about it at school, then promptly forgot all about it.)

And she finds that they don't dry out in her gravel beds either. The gravel will, like a children's sandpit, dry out on top and stay damp under the surface.

The bliss for the no-work-gardener with this system is that there are practically no weeds. Derry gets seedlings of *Cerinthe major* 'Purpurascens' and seedlings from her ash tree. Otherwise none. No weeds.

There are other advantages, too – little children can't use tricycles on gravel, and gravel is much more forgiving if you fall over on it. Comparing it with a bone-breaking fall on to stone flags, Derry calls it a 'comfortable fall'.

Derry has also experimented with a gravel bed 7.6 cm (3 in) deep. This one is effectively a raised bed, as it abuts a four-foot retaining wall. There, she finds that the plants are happy, but she does keep getting weeds and self-seeding in the shallower gravel. It's the sheer depth of the 20 cm (8 in) of gravel in the other bed that stops weed seeds being able to establish (12.7 cm (5 in) of gravel would probably do the trick and save a lot of back-breaking gravel lugging). But should you want self seeding, here's the trick. You'll just have to weed as well.

Choose your gravel with care ...

A gravel garden will need the gravel to be retained somehow – you must design it with edges, which could be a small stone or brick wall. You can't take it up next to grass, for both aesthetic and practical reasons – it will look too contrived without a boundary or a frame to it. It's also better to use a flat site, as on a slope you will gradually walk the gravel down and have to retrieve it, which is definitely not easy gardening. Initial terracing could make it work well on a slope.

You might like to choose a gravel that belongs in your locality and therefore looks at home in it – and this will possibly also make it easier to source. Contact a local delivery service and have them bring you the gravel from a local quarry. But do check what colour and type of gravel you will be getting, as even a local quarry may have different stone to that in your garden, depending on the geology. It is a good idea to go and look at the quarry to see what the stone is like and if you like the colour and shape of it. Besides, visiting a quarry is quite an adventure in itself. After that you are likely to need strong people with shovels and wheelbarrows ...

In some circumstances, with a little ingenuity at the edges, you may be able to turn the whole garden into a gravel garden. Think about it – no mowing, no paths to clear or weed, no small children on tricycles, just you and your plants.

... And your plants

Aesthetically, you don't just have a particular kind of plant to use – the alpine or Mediterranean – you also have a very particular and interesting look. These are plants that like light and air, so they are best planted with space around them. This gives you an unusual joy in a contemporary British garden: if they're not all massed together as in a conventional flowerbed, you can show off the form of a plant. Derry declares that ornamental grasses usually look stupid in a border – but they are the epitome of grace emerging from a gravel bed.

When the sun shines you will also potentially get the additional pleasure of scent – Mediterranean plants are often characteristically aromatic – think of cistus, salvias (apart from *Salvia sclarea* var. *turkestaniana*, which smells of untended armpits), agastache and herbs like thyme, rosemary, lavender and bay. You might add a grape vine such as 'Léon Millot' growing over a pergola and hope to swan around scoffing your own grapes one day.

You may have heard of, or come across Beth Chatto's Gravel Garden, which was also an experiment originally, designed to accommodate growing plants in a dry climate on a soil that was little more than gravel itself. I believe that gravel has been used differently there, principally as a mulch. It does involve weeding, and spreading mulch (rotted straw under shrubs – you can't mulch gravel). If you have similar conditions you may find the book, *Beth*

Chatto's Gravel Garden, helpful, as it will give you ideas and pictures for suitable planting.

DECKCHAIR TIP

Gravel gardens are for Mediterranean plants. If you have a longing for big, fat, coarse plants, this is not quite your style.

However, it's perhaps the only garden that can look good with a random collection of diverse plants. As long as they are ones that will be happy in Mediterranean conditions.

A SHRUB GARDEN

Shrubs take up a lot of space and once established will consume very little of your time and effort. If you leave enough space for them in the first place, you shouldn't need to prune most shrubs – just admire them. So, if you really don't want to do much gardening, you might like to create what used to be called a 'shrubbery'. Shrubberies have acquired a very poor reputation but I suspect that was more to do with the dubious activities people got up to in them rather than the things themselves. Though

I do remember reading an account by gardening writer Christopher Lloyd of designing a shrub border and wondering why on earth anyone would ever want to do anything so dull. It sounded very depressing. I think that was because his version had no intrinsic drama or excitement, no 'wow' factor, just a collection of worthy shrubs, arranged politely together. I think it's possible to do better.

It's not all about the flower ...

In my opinion, it's useful to start by focusing on foliage. Shrubs do have flowers, but they also have some pretty good foliage, which tends to make a contribution for much longer than most flowers. Green is not necessarily boring, it just sometimes needs noticing properly. But green is only a start – shrubs give you the chance to design with colour.

We have a shrub border: it's very dramatic and – to me – satisfying. It works for months with minimal attention. The shrubs are various, with the purples – *Cotinus* 'Grace', *Cercis canadensis* 'Forest Pansy' and *Acer palmatum* 'Atropurpureum' – and the silver *Elaeagnus*

'Quicksilver', which suckers and creeps about among the purples. I think this addition is what makes the planting, because it mixes the silver with the purple so well, instead of them all being separate. But it would still look pretty good even if they were all separate, because of the drama the colours offer. The *Elaeagnus* flowers inconspicuously but with an amazing scent that reaches around everywhere from the moment a few odd flowers appear. But flowers are not what this border is about.

All of these shrubs, apart from the *Acer*, can be cut down to the base or severely pruned if necessary to keep them lower and help manage the blending nicely. The suckering *Eleagnus* tries to escape out of the front, where it is cut to the ground in autumn. This has so far resulted in very small shrubs regrowing, which works well at the front with a few bronze fennel and other suitable perennials. I suppose if they get too vigorous I'll cut them down again mid-season. That'll show them.

To complete the ground covering (though now they have grown it hardly seems necessary) I added buddleia mint (*Mentha longifolia* 'Buddleia'), a grey-green mint that flowers at about the same time as a buddleia does, with a very similar – if much smaller – flower. This mint, as all mints, rampages around very satisfactorily when it's happy. Mint is ground cover on steroids, and a great, useful herb besides.

I hope this gives some idea of the dramatic possibilities of a shrubbery. You could be more subtle and simply mix good shades of one colour. Or you could think flowers and grow hydrangeas, because they flower for such a very long time. This is the one time when you could happily mix different hydrangeas with different colours and actually enjoy the result. You should know that the colours are different depending on whether your soil is acid or alkaline. You can get a little test tube test to play with to discover which yours is if you are in doubt but, personally, I think all the colours can be good. You might like to know in advance what they'll be though, if you're an impatient sort.

Or you could indulge an immoderate love of any other shrub, just bearing in mind different sizes and vigour when planting.

Roses, of course, are shrubs too. But they are not generally low maintenance and are singularly ugly in winter. If you love them, you could well make a garden of them and forget all else in your dedication and enthusiasm. In which case, make a pilgrimage to Mottisfont in Hampshire, where Graham Stuart Thomas designed the amazing rose garden. You'll soon forget those horrid, gawky, disease-prone hybrid teas and floribundas.

DECKCHAIR WISDOM

*Shrubs are currently quite unfashionable,
but this means that in a couple of years they will be
The Thing to have.*

This will make you feel very happy and superior.

What not to do in your garden in autumn

'In Heaven it is always autumn.'

John Donne

Autumn should really be time off. We all need to take a break and freshen our perceptions now and then. This is one of the best times of year to do that, before the garden media starts snowdropping us. Some people get aerated about their leaves and spend hours collecting and composting them. Always remember: leaves are for kicking and crunching as you walk on them.

Remove shading from the greenhouse.

Well, you never put any up in the first place, did you? And you are going to be so glad now that you don't have a greenhouse so you don't have to *clean* it! Oh, they do get grotty, and you never know when you might encounter a slimy slug or dead mouse. At least no one suggests dusting your greenhouse.

Prune rambling and climbing roses,
removing old and unproductive
stems and tying in new growth.

I always love this tip . . . My ramblers are growing up large trees and I do not propose to climb up a tree full of prickly rambler stems in order to try and cut some out and – remove them? As if. Nor would I want to bother with tying them in. Generally, ramblers manage to fasten themselves into a tree just fine: they're designed for it. Though I have had winter gales blow one rambler clean out of a tree, and that was some nightmare to deal with. All that very thorny growth had to be cut off and removed. Nasty.

And, tell me, why are we told to cut at an angle when we're pruning roses 'to prevent water getting into the cut area'? The stems will be at all sorts of different angles, so some of your slanty cuts will be dead upright, eager to catch some water. But, if you actually *tried* to get a drop of water to sit on that particular cut, bet your life it would keep running off.

You will, however, be pleased to know that cutting the bush in half with a hedge trimmer seems to work just as well as playing around with a pair of secateurs.

Shorten the stems of roses to reduce wind rock.

Bit of a nuisance, these roses, aren't they? Why do roses rock? Why doesn't every shrub and tree in your garden suffer from wind rock? Perhaps you'd better get out there and shorten the branches of your oak trees, your hydrangeas or your holly bushes – the hollies are evergreen so they'll catch the wind dreadfully, won't they? I don't think so.

Sow a green manure on bare ground to dig back into the soil.

Neither. Just mulch.

Plant bulbs in informal 'drifts' by throwing them down and planting where they land.

You'll only have to pick them up again when they don't land where you want them to. And I'm not sure that throwing them around does the bulbs much good. Neither do you wish to accidentally step on one, as it will either squish or send you flying. Put them in a bucket, and just wander and plant at will. They will come out at random. When I first planted daffodils in the meadow I thought 200 would go a long way. However, they looked pathetic. And worse – I'd planted them all singly, which really did look odd. They grow naturally in clumps and it's best to start them off that way, so that even if you don't have very many they do look as though they belong.

Ours have now, after thirty years, bulked up a bit, so they don't look so strange, and in fact some are overcrowded and a lot of them are coming up blind (i.e. not blooming). If I were dedicated and daft, I'd dig them up and replant. But I'm not. And the mystery to me is that when you see, as you do round here, a whole field full of the same wild daffodils flowering away like mad, you can be sure no one has been going round digging them up and sticking them back in. I was also told when I first planted bulbs, to plant them at the top of a hill, so they would spread by seeding down the slope. I now have a wonderful mass of crocuses, all at the top of the slope.

Keep deadheading your perennials.

I'll tell you yet another reason to be cautious about this. Once you get preoccupied with looking at the plants in search of the dying blooms, that is *all* you'll see. Gone are the happy days when you looked out at the garden and saw flowers. Now you'll see a job to be done: to go and search for the withering blooms and take them off in order for the plants to produce more flowers, which will only draw you out there looking for withering blooms again . . .

DECKCHAIR TIP

If you must deadhead, go out with a small battery hedge trimmer and chop them all off at once.

Chop down anything else you're finding depressing at the same time.

Plant up some small chrysanthemums in terracotta pots so they don't blow over.

They will blow over in the first autumn gale, and being terracotta, it'll be just your luck if they break.

Tidy up.

The house is for that.

Cover your pond with netting to stop leaves falling in and rotting.

Having rotting leaves in your pond is widely regarded as A Bad Thing, so we are supposed to net our ponds to keep them out. Not a single-person job, that, trying to throw the net right over the pond without it falling into the pond, and then managing to get to the other side to peg it down before it droops its way in. Some people have permanent netting anyway to protect their fish from heron, though you may think it's more exciting to attract and feed a few heron. I always feel extraordinarily privileged when we get a heron at the pond, though also anxious in case it pecks a hole in the liner. It can have the fish: the rest of the pond life would be better without them. Adding them was misguided.

I would think that the little creatures that live in your pond, like water beetles, the various larvae of caddisflies, hover flies, dragonflies, and wormy sorts of things would love the sludgy bottom. Indeed, frogs go and hibernate in it in winter if you give them a chance. It's true that ponds in the countryside seem to eventually fill up and disappear unless cleared out now and again, so I think it might be a good idea to have a clear-out of your pond every so often, when you think you'd like a nice smelly, squidgy job. But I have had a pond for over twenty years that has never been netted or cleaned. Wait till you can see the sludge, maybe? Or better still for the idle – do without water in the garden.

Hang wasp traps in fruit trees to stop wasps damaging the fruit.

Somehow they just don't get the message, do they?

Apply a bulky organic mulch around the base of trees, shrubs and climbers.

Well, if you must do something like this in November, be careful. If you get the mulch against the bark of the tree you'll rot it and do far more harm than good. But anyway – why would you be mulching in the cold and wet of November, for pity's sake? Any old time will do to mulch, in spite of a lot of nonsense talked about it. Mulch when it's warm, sunny and pleasant.

Fill in gaps in flower borders with small, pot-grown herbaceous perennials. They aren't expensive at this time of year and if planted now will make an impact in spring.

Never do this if you live anywhere with a tendency to wetness or rain: the plants will almost certainly rot off and waste your time and money. Though I suppose the compost from the pots and the rotted plant will add a little organic matter, and no harm in that.

DECKCHAIR TIP

Don't have gaps in your flowerbeds – grow vigorous thuggy plants.

If you have a gap, use it as a place for the grass mowings.

Cover outdoor furniture or, if you have space, move it into a sheltered spot to reduce the amount of damage over the next few months.

If you're daft enough to have outdoor furniture that can't live outside (aren't we all?), a sheltered spot won't help. Rot is the problem, and 'shelter' doesn't mean 'dry' in this climate. Though covering could be useful.

Fit spiral rabbit guards to protect trunks and stems – rabbits are likely to become a problem in many areas now that temperatures are falling.

If you have rabbits and didn't do this when you planted the things (whatever they are) you might as well go and dig them up now. They'll already be chomped – rabbits like to sample the new things you put out for them. But it's true that if the weather is really bad, as in frost and, particularly, snow, you may find that your lovely old holly tree, far too fat for a tree guard, may get barked by

ravenous rabbits. Wire netting could protect it if you're feeling very vulnerable about a favourite tree. Remember to take it quite high up though, since the rabbits may be using a snow lift.

Rake the dead leaves off the lawn.

If you are really stuck for something to do and you're desperate for a bit of harmless exercise you might have a go. Otherwise, wait for the wind to blow them on to the beds, where they will be useful mulch, or, if you must, mow them up and dump the mowings on to said beds for same purpose. And forget leaf mould, with elaborate containers for leaves to rot in or the alternative ugly bin bags. It's a waste of time and effort when you can simply put leaves straight on to your beds and borders (no, not *that* bed – the one outside) to the same effect.

Keep on top of weeds.

Put piles of mown leaves on top of them and hope they'll all rot.

Plant bare-root trees and shrubs.

Avoid buying bare-root plants – these are the ones wrapped in newspaper instead of sitting happily in a pot.

I've never had much joy from them, and plants in pots can stay in the pots for a good while if you can't face the great outdoors. Plants in pots don't ever need heeling in, unlike bare-root plants, which is excellent since it's never possible to find anywhere to do it. However, plants in pots do sometimes get pot-bound, and they may never grow out of that spiralling round and round that that induces. So if there's any chance this has happened, wash all the potting compost off and plant bare root. I know what I just said – but this time you plant straight away and when you're ready.

And while we're at it, make sure you plant them straight into your garden soil. Don't add fertilizer and don't add other organic matter. The latest science shows that the sooner they grow into whatever they are going to be living in the better. The only time you add extra fertilizer is if you've done a soil test and you're short of something identified, and in that case you presumably have the whole garden to worry about, not just this tree.

DECKCHAIR WISDOM

The whole of gardening really consists of planting things – then cutting them down.

Plant out spring bedding displays of pansies, violas and primulas.

We don't do bedding – too much like hard work. You might buy one in a pot for your windowsill though, if you need cheering up.

Continue to lift dahlia tubers, begonias and gladiolus corms to store dry over the winter months. Remove the dead foliage before storing.

This is not a job for you. If you'd really like such plants, grow them as annuals and get some new ones next year. A different colour perhaps? They don't cost more than a bunch of flowers and flower a lot longer.

Other important things

SEATS

One of the things that makes me a little sad is people asking if we ever sit on the seats in the garden. For me, the garden is for enjoying and one of our favourite enjoyments is to have a drink together in the garden before supper. This can have certain dire consequences for the cooking (my husband, Charles, tells me he positively enjoys the black bits) but it is the perfect time to stop and sit. The light's often at its best at that time of day, and if there has been a wind it is surprising how often it drops then and goes quiet. So the trick is to have as many seats in the garden as you can fit in. They make a great focal point as well as a sitting place.

However, one of the problems with having many seats is that if they are wood, and most of the best are, they will need constant repair and repainting (I like colourful seats), sometimes even those that optimistically call themselves 'hardwood'. Hardwood seems to magically become softwood all by itself. Paint is supposed to help prevent this, though I suspect that it actually somehow manages to encourage it. Metal seats, of course, rust. The other difficulty I've had with seats we've bought is that they tend to be the wrong shape and size. They will be too far off the ground for anyone a little short to comfortably rest their feet, and not deep enough to be able to lean back comfortably. So I designed my own and, like a few things in this book, they involve a bit of initial work, which will then pay off for years. They are based on breeze blocks – and you can get a builder to do all the work, of course.

The breeze blocks form the back of the seat and you (or the builder) can cut the blocks to make the back in whatever shape appeals to you. These seats don't move, so choose your spot well and then build the back, with a foundation to keep it standing – that's a trench rather bigger than the seat back filled with concrete. Then at the front of this back (as ever, this is easier to do than describe) make two – or three, if it's a very big seat – small breeze block 'arms' to the height you want the seat to be. Which may be much lower than normal, or higher maybe if you've got to the point in life when getting up out of a seat is the biggest challenge.

This bit of the construction will also give you the front to back depth of the seat, since the next bit of the construction is to get some wooden planks laid across these supports to make your seat bit. We were very posh and got our local joiner to make the seats to size in hardwood and to fit them. (Sad to say, that after many years, one is showing signs of a little rot in the corner. I tell you this in the interest of strict and slightly sad honesty.) You screw these planks into the supports. I recommend that you make this front to back deep enough for you to lie down on the seat in case you approach it sometime after a bit of reckless weeding and need a quick lie down to recover. And you will also find that although the angle between the seat and the back is a right angle, you will still be able to comfortably lean back if the seat is deep front to back. Which is necessary. The days of sitting up straight are long gone, especially if you are having a drink or two. Make the seat bit big enough to accommodate a tray with drinks and nibbles on as well as other people.

Then your builder renders the breeze blocks and you paint them any colour of your choice, as long as it's not green. Green things never look right against nature's greens and I wish manufacturers of hose ends and other similar bits of garden plastic would learn that. White is a bit startling too. But you may want to startle someone.

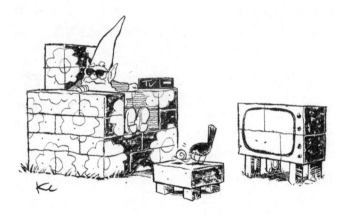

And then there you are. You will need to repaint the back and seat supports now and again, but masonry paint on a flat surface is a whole different game than painting wood. And the painting is purely decorative rather than that nasty business of trying to stop the rot. Unless, of course, you've done like me and painted words on to the back of the seat which are then impossible to paint round. Or if you have discovered a little rot in your wooden hardwood planks. In which case, a little wood hardener will be useful. Worst comes to the worst, a plank is easy to replace.

Then sit on it. Often.

DECKCHAIR WISDOM

Comfortable seats are essential if you're going to go outside for pleasure at all.

So if your seats worry you because they rot, or make you fidget because you're never comfortable, you do need to make changes.

WATERING

I'm inclined to suggest that in the UK it's absurd to ever water your lawn, since it will green up again as soon as it rains (which will be when the government gets round to appointing a Minister for Drought). But I have visited the south-east of the country in quite an ordinary summer and seen grass going yellow and the borders in gardens open to the public also looking miserable and parched.

Ordinarily, I would say that it's only new planting that will need watering but I have to have some sympathy for people with this problem, especially in parts of the country with very high levels of population and thus too little water for everyone. It is a mystery to me why we've never discovered a better way of disposing of our waste than washing it away in water treated to drinking quality, but I don't imagine anyone is about to remedy that. So I can only sympathize with anyone who finds their plants wilting in a hose pipe ban.

There are things that can be done to ameliorate the effects of drought, but I wouldn't want to pretend they will save you *in extremis*. However, for the rest of us, with plenty of rain and regularly suffering from flooding, making hollow laughter noises at the idea of drought, there are ways to see that your plants make the best of the water and will survive a little absence of it. The most obvious tip is that boring old thing: mulching. Mulching will help to stop what water there is in the soil from evaporating, and it will help to add humus to your soil, which is a good thing. Don't ask me what exactly humus is, as it seems no one precisely knows, but we know soil and plants need it and that it has a kind of spongy effect, helping the soil retain moisture. So: mulch. You know you should and it will please you to be spared the sight of weed-hungry, bare soil.

If you're going to do it, do it right

If you really have to water and the powers that be have not forbidden it, you can ignore advice about when you must do it. Water does not scorch plants if applied in sunlight (or you would have noticed the effects in April, when sun and showers still follow each other relentlessly and reassuringly). You can read a lot about the different watering needs of different kinds of soil, but, hey – are you really going to get serious about stuff like that? Hardly. They say if you're going to do it, do it thoroughly, which is good advice, but I find it hard to believe that plants are better off with no water than a little in desperate times (it's not like your too-light watering will send roots shooting up to the surface, never to seek water lower down again).

I'm guessing that standing in the garden watering with a spray on the end of a hose is likely to have you giving up too quickly, as soon as you remember that you should be sitting in the garden with a drink for yourself in your hand, not a hose. The dreaded sprinkler will keep at it longer than you can face, and you can even get ones that make pretty spraying patterns to admire as you enjoy your drink. What you are supposed to do with the stale contents of a water butt I have no idea, but if you have a small garden and a hosepipe ban you'll be chuffed you've got it. You could fill 150 water butts of 160-litre capacity in a reasonably wet year from the rainwater off your roof, even in the south-east of the UK. Maybe you could just fill your garden with water butts instead of plants and flog the water to your neighbours in a drought?

Finally, don't bother with hanging baskets. If you are serious about taking gardening easy, don't have plants in pots and definitely no houseplants, which are just gardening indoors.

DECKCHAIR WISDOM

Our ridiculous habit of using vast quantities of purified water to flush our loos has led to some strange attitudes and an occasional need to ration the blessed stuff.

Campaign for a new method of waste disposal – there has to be a better way and we may even be able to return to using our waste as fertilizer.

COMPOST

Many gardens contain a shrine, a site of strange rituals. It's called a compost heap and is generally considered an essential component of a garden. It may, however, be completely superfluous.

We have this idea that the soil is like a ravenous baby, demanding to be fed every minute and bound to cause big trouble if we neglect the poor thing. And, like a baby, soil doesn't talk, so if something appears to be wrong our likely first attempt at a remedy is to stuff it with food. With both baby and soil that can be a serious mistake.

Compost is often seen as the ideal medium to provide this extra nourishment and so we get ourselves a heap. And often with it, a heap of trouble, since it is as much trouble to look after as the aforesaid baby. Though in the case of a compost heap, unlike a baby, you may be encouraged to pee on it. And turn it regularly with a pitchfork.

So are our garden soils ravenous? In this country, in the average garden, that is very unlikely unless you are growing vegetables, soft fruit or annuals, where you will be tending to take some of the goodness away all the time as crops.

Do you really need to feed?

You will probably never need to feed your soil with any nutrients at all. You really shouldn't trouble yourself with the expense and effort of buying special plant foods and administering them to the ground – it will probably be happier without them and more importantly, it could get an overdose. Which is not much better for the soil than overdoses are for people. If you believe you may have a soil deficiency, get a soil test before you try to rectify it. Your plant may be poorly rather than starving – and may well grow out of whatever it is if you let it. Yellowing in a plant may be due to cold, waterlogging, drought, iron deficiency or perhaps to a virus. You can see that you might do best to let the plant die and have a nice funeral then try something else. The hands-off approach applies as much to compost as to artificial fertilizers – it contains nutrients and your soil may be full up of them.

I think this may be one of the hardest things for you to credit. In advertising it is said that you need to see an advert three times before it actually registers with you, and it's probably the same with unusual advice. You are endlessly told to compost, make a heap, turn a heap . . . and worse – to spend money on your heap. It used to be simple – you made a couple of big containers – as big as you could manage and find space for, filled them with degradable stuff and then alternated between rotting and using. There was always an initial wait for the rot to happen, which is where the compost-turning probably began. Or else the object of that miserable exercise may have been to see if that was where your potato peeler ended up.

If disposing of kitchen waste is the issue, your local council will happily take all your kitchen waste away for you, for the cost, in our parish, of walking to the gate with the bin every week and then fetching it back when they've emptied it. Simples.

Larger garden waste can also be removed by the council at a price, and so that may require a bin. But whether it's your lawn mowings or the dead stalks from your flower beds that you need to get rid of, there are better alternatives than parting with money every time.

Lawn mowings may be best dealt with by using a mulching mower, which returns the cuttings, suitably chopped up, back to your lawn to feed it. (Sigh.) As you are taking grass off all the time, food for the lawn may be necessary. On the other hand, I have neither mulched nor fed our grass (best call it grass – lawn might be a bit too posh) in nearly thirty years and it's still green and still growing. I have, up to now, used the mowings as mulch wherever I had a bare patch in my borders where otherwise weeds might appear. In all that time I have been gradually making a four-acre garden, so I have had a lot of bare earth to cover and protect from weeds as I have slowly progressed. I pile the cuttings on the beds – without rotting them first – and in a very short time they resemble that much-admired material, manure.

In the early days, with yards and yards of bare soil, I also needed wood chip to mulch the beds, and I still use it in places as an extra. I first used to get bark from the local fencing company, since then I have managed to get supplies of chippings from tree surgeons. Both have been perfect mulches, suppressing weeds, helping to retain moisture and protect the soil, and adding a slow feed to the plants. Despite persistent rumours, chippings and bark do *not* take nitrogen from the soil. I know – you will need to read that three times before believing it, so I have here to recommend you look up Linda Chalker-Scott, who gives *only* science-based advice, for your second take on that particular piece of wisdom. I'm not sure about the third, as pseudo-science seems to spread like weeds on an un-mulched plot. I was horrified, somewhat naively, to read a well-respected gardening expert saying in a popular magazine this untrue thing about nitrogen robbing the soil.

Let it rot!

As my beds have filled up I have begun to have ready mulch. In the autumn I cut down all the herbaceous growth in the beds and borders (whatever the difference between those two may be). We leave the debris on the beds then as the mulch. Some people, used to the sight of bare soil, which now gives me the horrors, will find this an odd look. They may prefer to do the lately fashionable thing and leave the dying foliage until spring, so that birds may enjoy the seeds and you may enjoy the hoar frost effect on said foliage. If you have followed Piet Oudolf's dictum that a plant is only any use if it looks good when dying back, you may be grateful you held back. But if you live in a wet part of the UK like some of us you may find it all turning into a soggy mess and wish you'd cut it all off in the autumn.

Both have their merits and demerits. If you leave it until spring you can often save yourself having to cut and can jump up and down on the by-then brittle foliage instead, which will also give you plenty of useful exercise. Don't do that on the foliage of ornamental grasses, though, especially on a slope – it can get wonderfully slippery and send you flying. As for the bird food, I enjoy seeing the birds pick through the autumn-cut foliage, so I have no reason to suppose they wish it were still standing up. (Though it has to be said that the lazy items do seem to spend more time getting seeds for minimum effort at the birdfeeder. They have obviously been reading this book . . .) There are also no doubt little creepy beasties of various sorts hiding in the debris of the cut down foliage and also getting picked out by the birds. Who can tell if that is good or bad?

You may wonder why I don't do as you are usually advised to do and cart all this stuff off to the compost heap to rot down, so that I may amuse myself some months later bringing it all back. In case that is not obvious – it rots down happily all by itself *in situ*. I have cared for my plants and soil this way for nearly thirty years and the results recommend the practice. It may be my very best, worth the price of this book, advice. Try it and see. Maybe just once if it seems very drastic – just to try it? If you hate the look – add some chippings on the top. If you must.

If you do grow vegetables you may well find compost useful even if it will, inevitably, be full of extra weed seeds. Vegetable gardening is much harder work even if you don't do unnecessary things. It's just part of the price of that rather expensive, in time and effort, activity. If you do grow vegetables you will need to keep the soil covered, just like everywhere else, but you might just be best to do that with compost or other organic (preferably weed-free) mulch.

Here I return to Charles Dowding for experience and knowledge of compost heaps. Charles, who runs courses on easy gardening, says that his students start to get all excited when they get to the compost bit. You can picture them all at the bins, jumping up and down . . . Firstly, Charles tells us he puts any old weed in his compost, couch grass, bindweed, ground elder, the lot. So that's one less job for you, sorting your compost offerings. He also adds blighted stems and leaves from his tomatoes and potatoes. (Yes, even the great Charles Dowding gets blighted – that's what comes of experimenting.) He points out that blight grows on living plant tissue not the dead bits in your heap.

He also doesn't think your heap needs to get hot, which was once regarded as the absolute desiderata of compost management. He clearly takes the temperature of his heap, and believes 35 to 40 degrees centigrade is ideal. Above that, like the stuff that comes from your local authority offerings and which has been well cooked, it is, he believes, pretty lifeless.

In case you still have the slightest interest, Charles only turns his heaps once and believes that makes it a little bit better, by adding air. He does also seem to think it will be fine without, and as it's used spread as a mulch, you'd think that spreading would get the air in. If you want to grow vegetables properly you clearly have much research and many critical decisions to make and frankly, I don't envy you any of it.

DECKCHAIR TIP

In spite of all temptation, if you want an easy life let your council compost for you.

But if that doesn't work for you, make a cheap compost bin from used pallets and do it the Charles Dowding way. Then invite his students to come and be all excited by your compost.

WEEDS

Weeds do separate the good organic people from the less good 'lean on the odd chemical' types like me. Mulching makes weeding easier for all of us – both worthy and unworthy – not just by stopping most annual weeds from germinating or finding bare soil to seed in, but in making the ground softer and easier to remove a weed from. Somehow, the mulch also 'presents' the weed better too, especially early in the year (plants seem to grow more separate and discrete in a mulch). This also, we chemical types must confess, makes them easier to zap. I have been zapping with glyphosate since I began the garden, and I know that my garden could not have been made without it. Hand-weeding two acres is not feasible with just two part-time people, and an early garden has lots of available spaces for weeds.

But then nothing dates a book quite as quickly as its chemicals. Where has Covershield gone? Or Casoron G? My parents swore by that to keep their paths clear. What about Weedex or, indeed, sodium chlorate? It's a bit like mentioning a floppy disk – these are names that date you and the books that mention them. So, probably, will glyphosate one day soon. I believe it is already illegal in some countries: the European Food Safety Authority, which advises EU policymakers, says that glyphosate is unlikely to cause cancer but the World Health Organization's International Agency for Research on Cancer has classified glyphosate as '*probably* carcinogenic to humans', along with baby oil, tea bag manufacturing, cooked meat and fish, grapefruit juice, aloe vera, cinnamon and coconut oil . . .

I do believe that some people are organic by nature – all their instincts demand it. They feel that Satan is sitting in a huge tower block commanding his minions to poison the human race and all life on the planet as fast as possible. And some people are sceptical by nature, basically idle and hoping to get away with it before all chemicals bar water are totally eliminated (which, on reflection, would also destroy all life on the planet).

Anyway, today a sceptic like me can still get away with chemical assistance. A small hand sprayer filled with glyphosate is my tool of choice on a sunny spring day (I can hear those cries of horror). Thankfully, now that the garden is well filled as well as well mulched, there won't be much need for this exercise later in the year if I manage that one spring afternoon of weedkilling.

I do occasionally search for an alternative, without finding anything convincing. I know that glyphosate is safer and more thoroughly tested than most of the household remedy weedkillers that sometimes get promoted as 'organic', like vinegar and salt, both of which *are* illegal to use as weedkillers. The fact that you can eat something doesn't make it good for the soil, and that something is harmless to the soil doesn't make it good to drink. Sadly, it has to be pointed out – because I do know that the organics are good people – that any garden cure you can make at home, happily believing that household items are familiar and safe, is likely to do more harm than a well-tested commercial product, it being untested for whatever plan you have in mind. And it will be illegal. It's hard to be good.

Embrace your weeds

Still, some of us make life a little easier for ourselves by adopting some of our weeds and cultivating them. I have just used glyphosate in an attempt to kill off the many grasses that are trying to grow out of my bed of ground elder (*Aegopodium podagraria*). It is a pleasing small patch of this plant with the classy, glossy leaf and a pretty white flower, which is very much like the fashionable *Ammi majus* (described by Sarah Raven, who is a proper expert, as having 'lacy, white flowers, like a more delicate form of cow parsley'). If you are searching for good-looking, robust and happily spreading ground cover, look no further. Ground elder doesn't seem to spread by seed, so if you can contain your patch with a tough hedge or path, it will look very pleasing for months. After flowering, cut it right to the base and it will soon shine again.

A great many of our so-called weeds have attractive flowers. Some call cow parsley (*Anthriscus sylvestris*) a weed, along with the common poppy (*Papaver rhoeas*), field bindweed (*Convolvulus arvensis*) – which I have attempted to establish in my garden without success several times – and the pretty blue speedwell (*Veronica chamaedrys*), for example. Call them 'wild flowers', though, and we'll all be permitted to enjoy them. I wouldn't be without the dandelions in our meadow, for their cheerful yellow blobs, along with the wonderful meadow buttercup (*Ranunculus acris*). Our neighbour's field was once a whole wonderful carpet of buttercups, until they destroyed the lot for nothing more than to let a couple of horses graze. And would any of us seriously wish to be without a few daisies?

Some weeds are edible, such as common sorrel (*Rumex acetosa*), dandelion (*Taraxacum officinale*) and nettle (*Urtica dioica*). And some are EVIL, like Japanese knotweed (*Fallopia japonica*), which can reduce the value of your house. I think the thing is to know your weed, consider it well and then decide its fate. At the last resort, no plant can survive being perpetually deprived of light. Constant execution or cover will see them off if you have the patience of a saint.

DECKCHAIR WISDOM

If you loathe the sight of a weed, then you need to have a garden where they are both obvious and easy to get rid of.

A gravel garden may be just what you always needed.

What not to do in your garden in winter

'No animal, according to the rules of animal-etiquette, is ever expected to do anything strenuous, or heroic, or even moderately active during the off-season of winter.'

(Kenneth Grahame, *The Wind in the Willows*)

If you're lucky, your garden will be smothered in snow all winter, thus keeping it warm – snow does act as a super insulating blanket – and keeping you snugly indoors, admiring the view. Garden pundits will tell you it's time to read seed catalogues, deciding what to sow. *You* will put them in the recycling bin and find more exciting things to do.

Collect leaves from underneath any rose bushes that had blackspot or rust last summer and burn them (the leaves, presumably) to reduce the possibility of re-infection.

Well, this is not a jolly job for a cold December day, is it? Unless a little bonfire might warm you up – assuming local regulations and consideration of your neighbours permits burning soggy debris. What are the chances you'd get away with no re-infection? Very little would be my guess. I believe susceptible roses will just keep on getting diseased and laugh at you unless you also use noxious chemicals regularly and have lots of luck. But if you do believe anything could make a difference, it might be worth adding some mulch (preferably not composed of diseased rose leaves) over the fallen leaves and smothering them. Slightly less bending involved. Definitely less desperate than trying to light a fire with wet leaves.

Group plants in pots together in a sheltered place to help prevent root damage from frost.

One really hard frost and you'll wish you'd stayed indoors and saved your back. If you insist, do wear gloves as you may otherwise have a nasty encounter with a slimy slug snoozing under the rim of the pot.

To improve drainage and reduce waterlogging, stand planted patio pots up on feet so that they are slightly raised from direct contact with the ground.

Here's fun: buy many, many pot feet at great expense, or make some (er, how)? Lift pots with one hand and arrange feet in correct positions on the ground where you will be replacing the pot. Try them for fit. Pot falls over. Pick it up and rearrange the feet; replace pot. Get dustpan and brush to clear up compost spill from fallen-over pot; replace compost in pot. Move on to the next pot. I live in the wet west of the country and am not aware of any of my container plants suffering as a result of the pot sitting right on the ground. They do sometimes acquire worms but they are no trouble.

Plant up containers with layers of bulbs and add hardy cyclamen, evergreen grasses and ivy for winter colour.

Oh, here comes one of those dreadful depressing containers with fifty different plants and a dressing of crisp packets and fag ends.

DECKCHAIR TIP

Don't grow any plants in pots. If you do accidently find you have some plants in pots, throw them away in autumn when they've finished flowering.

Take cuttings of ...

Stop right there. That is gardening for the serious and committed, not you.

Rough-dig empty borders and let the frost and worms break the clods of soil up.

What are you doing with empty borders? Get them planted up instead! We know that digging is bad for the soil, so leave that out. You'll be glad to hear that I've tried seeing if frosts and worms break up clumps of soil. My soil is not especially claggy, but it didn't work. Claggy lumps appear to have a very long shelf life and great resistance to frost and worms.

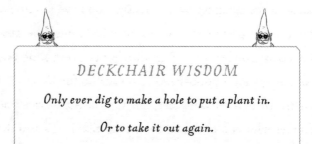

DECKCHAIR WISDOM

Only ever dig to make a hole to put a plant in.

Or to take it out again.

Check newly planted perennials and shrubs in case heavy rain has exposed the roots. If so, add soil or compost over the roots to protect them.

This is called mulching by more enlightened people. If you keep everything permanently mulched, checking for rampant roots is redundant

Winter-prune your wisteria, cutting back summer side shoots to two or three buds.

A wisteria is not a plant for us. It has to be pruned twice a year and usually grows against a wall, so it needs tying in to things you have to insert into said wall before you can start the tying in. Subsequently, you have to remove the ties you previously tied on to these things, because the ties are rotting, strangling the shoots, preventing you from pruning the shoots and so on and so forth.

And then it flowers after all that effort – and you wonder why you bothered for a plant that looks as if the flowers were placed in the washing machine at the wrong temperature and have faded very badly. Unless you have a white wisteria, but even then, is it worth all that effort?

DECKCHAIR WISDOM

Don't grow wisteria.

Or any plant which needs attaching to a wall.

Dig up the leeks and parsnips you have left and heel them in to a trench beside a convenient path. They will keep well for several months like this and can easily be brought indoors when you want them.

OK, how many things are you now having to do in order to save yourself buying a few veggies? And after growing the blessed things, you now have to dig them all up and – then *replant* them! So, do you have a nice place all ready and waiting, soil all empty and friable – and right next to a convenient path – in which to plant them more loosely than they were before? I take it that's what's meant by heeling in in this context. And then they are brought in easily? By rushing out and digging them up in the cold, dark and wet when you've just realized you need them for dinner? We'll draw a veil over your veg supply when it snows . . .

Word to the wise: if you must grow a leek, forget about digging it up in the snow – just let it go on and flower. Astonishingly nice flower.

Cover heavy clay soil with polythene to keep it drier and allow winter digging.

Now here's a new one. Just suppose you are mad enough to dig (just *don't*), you now have to buy polythene and flap about with that too. It doesn't just lie down tidily, you know, wherever you ask it to. It will fold over where you don't want it, trip you up, blow up into your face and then refuse to stay laid down. Mad.

Avoid walking on your lawn when it is frosted or covered in snow, as this will damage the grass beneath.

This is very strange. I have done this – walked on grass in snow and frost – and never seen the slightest evidence of damage after. Just saying.

Knock snow off your hedges to prevent damage.

I have spent many hours when I might have been admiring a beautiful snow scene or even sledging, knocking snow off our many beautiful hedges. However, I got fed up with the way the snow always ended up going down the back of my neck and into my boots, and so during the last few snowfalls I haven't bothered, even with our yew hedges, which I have seen bowed down and horribly bent under heavy snow. I then prepared myself for bad damage, knowing I deserved it. In the event, though, they somehow put themselves right again. I can't be sure they'd do that after weeks of really heavy snow, so you may have to make your own judgement here. But I'm not rushing out there in the snow again.

before

after

Kc

Keep clearing up any leaves so that slugs and snails can't shelter beneath them.

This is the kind of thing that could truly drive us all mad. Slugs and snails will *never* have a problem finding somewhere to live. They don't need estate agents or help from anyone. They even live in huge quantities safely underground. There are thousands of them in your garden (truly) and none of them are wondering where to sleep.

Remove old hellebore leaves to make the flowers more visible as they emerge in spring.

This is an interesting one, because some people tell you to remove the leaves in order to reduce the likelihood of the fungus hellebores get, *Coniothyrium hellebori*, or to increase light and air, which the fungus will supposedly dislike. As I mentioned earlier, when I get the same advice with different explanations, I get suspicious. I wonder if this expert is inventing a plausible explanation for doing something they've been told to do, and no doubt conscientiously do, while really not having the faintest idea of why. And most experts will tell you to remove any diseased leaves – the ones with black fungus blotches – presumably to stop the fungus spreading.

I am never sure that I like the effect of the flowers standing all starkly naked with no leaves at all. I used to do as I was told and removed the leaves but then looked at the flowers when they arrived and thought they would have looked better with some of the handsome leaves to set them off. So now I leave the leaves on some of mine, even the ones with horrible black fungus marks (because I'm too busy/lazy/distracted to go round cutting them off – they don't pull readily).

Some of my other hellebore leaves get strimmed off and left on the bed to rot, because that's the easiest way to care for the beds and because they make a useful, if maybe fungus-ridden, mulch. I do this in November (truthfully, latterly, Jeff the Gardener does it) – I think earlier would be losing whatever feeding benefit the leaves offer, and even this late it may be costly to the plants. But they seem to do all right. Sometimes they return in robust black-spot-free health. And sometimes they get black spots on the leaf. And sometimes deer chomp the flowers off anyway and it all seems very sad. So it's not obvious what to suggest you might do. Perhaps whatever you prefer?

Cut back damaged, diseased and the oldest stems of brightly coloured willows and thin, overcrowded stems.

That would be a very silly thing to do, as this is the time of year when you are supposed to be admiring their alien and rather lurid effect.

Try forcing rhubarb plants by placing an upturned bucket or bin over the crown. This will force tender pink stems to grow that will be ready in about eight weeks.

Rhubarb is something I always intend to eat but it's a bit of a faff, even if you buy it. After all, you can't just chew on even the tender pink stems – you have to cook them. And we don't have puddings anymore, except for when we have friends over. So I've never done the bucket trick, in spite of the fact we have a clump of rhubarb we inherited when we came here. It comes back every year and is an attractive foliage plant until it begins to look manky, at which point I pull off the leaves and dispose of them. They are very big leaves: I have always wondered how they fit in these buckets people stick on top of them. I'd imagine they'd resent it. Or go on growing and emerge showing off a sort of bucket hat. One day, when I have nothing better to do and can't afford to buy any rhubarb should I fancy some, I will experiment with a bucket.

Start to think about your hanging baskets for this year. Order your fuchsias, geraniums and lobelia now in preparation for spring.

I'm afraid I have a horror of hanging baskets except outside pubs. I know, it's a snob thing. They might even be quite exciting if you experimented with perhaps one very beautiful plant with leaves and form that show off well, trailing over the edge of a baskety thing. But for the time-constrained, which is us, it is best to avoid the challenges of planting into a basket (which is principally holey), having added something to stop everything falling through the holes, then feeding, watering and hanging up the said contraption. Go and admire the ones hanging outside the pub over a pint or three.

Wash empty pots by scrubbing them with hot water and a mild detergent. Rinse them well afterwards.

This is mad. You want to bring indoors all those hundreds of pots you have acquired and hidden around the place under benches and behind the shed? They are all very dirty and have cobwebs on them. You want to wash all that down your sink? And then arrange endless flowerpots on your draining board, since you really cannot quite bring yourself to use a tea towel and dry several dozen flowerpots with bits of compost still lurking in the recesses?

I used to wash flowerpots, outside, with a hose and a washing-up brush. And yes, I would hose myself down, too. And yes, I would get freezing cold. And yes, the blighters wouldn't stay still and be washed. I gave up and have used dirty pots for years – with no evidence of any harm at all to anything but the spiders that get dislodged whenever I need a flowerpot.

Repair and re-shape lawn edges.

Lawn edges are one of the ugliest things to ever have found their way into people's gardens. They not only display the equally unfortunate wiggles that people will cut out of their lawns in the misguided belief that wiggles look 'natural', but they oblige you to discipline your plants and keep them off your neat edges. Some people like them, apparently, so if you need advice about them, try those people.

But I'm here to tell you that it's not a good look and, anyway, a more genuinely natural look is now fashionable. Your garden now should appear a little more shaggy at the edges, relaxed and comfortable. Like you, if you abandon edging. Grow vigorous plants along the edges instead and let them fight it out. I use *Alchemilla mollis* and it works like a dream, requiring only a once-a-year mow or strim when it's finished flowering. It bounces back into leaf a week later and continues to keep the grass edge tidy.

Dig a trench for runner beans and fill with rotted compost from your compost bin. Then during winter you can carry on adding kitchen waste. In late spring cover with soil and sow your beans on top.

I must confess that we do sometimes grow runner beans, from plants usually bought in a garden centre and planted in the same place they were planted last year, with no improvement to the soil or additions of rotted vegetables or mythical compost. In a poor year (i.e. incessant torrential rain) we get a few meals' worth of runner beans. In a good year, we get far too many and fret about wasting them. We have no desire to feed the local foxes with food debris or provide local cats with a free loo, so – no trenches.

Newly planted trees and shrubs should be protected from the wind by erecting a shelter around them.

This is another construction for the gales or snow to destroy. And, of course, the shelter will just catch the wind and bring the whole lot down.

Lay old carpeting or similar over cold frames to protect them.

Er, isn't part of the point of a cold frame to let light to the plants while protecting them from cold? Will this mean rushing in and out removing and replacing sodden wet pieces of carpet? With slugs on? You're joking, right?

This is a good time to prune many things.

Generally speaking, you could do well to remember a couple of pruning thoughts. The first is to prune when you feel like it, if you must, and the second is to prune flowering things after they've finished flowering, if you must. Except hydrangeas, which you should leave until spring. The prune-after-flowering doesn't apply either to fruit trees, where you would be cutting off the fruit, or roses if you want the heps or hips. (They mean the same but heps does stop you imagining a rose bush with its hands on its hips.)

But there are one or two flowering things you could prune after they have finished flowering. But really, unless they are too big, have ugly or huge dead flowers or are a funny shape, I'm not sure why you'd bother. You can go over your rose bushes, should you have some, with a hedge trimmer, sometime between autumn and spring. And if you're wondering whether you should prune your heathers, I'd chop them down to the ground and be done with the sad things unless you live somewhere like the Scottish Highlands, where they look right and feel happy.

Plant things.

You're often told to plant or move things at this time of year, while they are dormant. (Not that evergreens are dormant at this time of year, just to confuse you.) The advice usually says to do this when the ground is neither frozen nor waterlogged. As it will inevitably be one or the other in winter, I shouldn't bother. I have moved things at all times of year with no ill effects – though I do live in a wet part of the world. Playing mobile shrubs in a drought means a lot of watering is in order should you rashly decide to do such a thing, but it can be done if the shrub is little. Herbaceous plants seem to move any old time if subsequently kept wet, and for me it helps if I can see them in the first place. So winter is not the favoured time.

However, if you do decide to plant a tree, you shouldn't really stake it. If it is bare-rooted and biggish (like as tall as you) then you may need to – but stake as low as you can and remove the stake as soon as possible. Never leave it longer than a year. Use something soft and with some give to fasten the stake to the tree.

Why? Because trees need to wave about in the wind – it helps them thicken their trunks and anchor their roots.

Teaches them, you know, to stand up for themselves. And besides – everyone forgets the stake and the tie until they notice with horror how they've been strangling the poor thing. Far better not to stake at all.

Prepare seed beds for vegetables by removing all weeds and forking in plenty of compost.

Never fork in any compost. That sort of disturbance destroys the mycorrhizal-root network. (Bet that shut you up.) But we know that by now, don't we? *No* digging. Use compost or compost plus wood chip as mulch on your veggie beds, if you must have them (compost or veggie beds).

Soak sweet pea seeds overnight before sowing them.

In the good old days when I grew sweet peas from seed and battled endlessly and horribly with mice, I found they germinated quite happily unsoaked (the sweet peas, not the mice). But now we buy sweet pea plants ready grown and plant them out in April. I'm sorry to say in the same old place without any fertilizer, compost (well, once, maybe, when the mood took him), or any other encouragement. We don't take them to the local flower show for prizes but we get some good vases full. In truth, sweet pea-picking, having to be done daily to keep them going, can become a bit of a chore. Not for the truly idle gardener perhaps.

Winter-prune gooseberries.

As if! Have you seen the thorns on a gooseberry bush? Pity those poor babies born underneath.

DECKCHAIR WISDOM

Winter is really for staying indoors warm and cosy, watching the weather through glass. If you're tempted outdoors, try a good book?

THE WINTER GARDEN

If you are misguided enough to read garden magazines at Christmas, you will not only find them discussing snowdrops (they always get the months wrong, it's the law) but someone will have been out counting the number of flowers that are out in the garden on Christmas Day. They (the flowers) will probably be looking somewhat bedraggled, having been attacked by winter weather, but each one is equivalent to a star stamp in the Boy's Own Stamp Collection. And the Best Boy is the one with the most. It's like the infinite variety of snowdrops with infinitesimal differences from each other – possessing these things makes you a winner. So there's lots of competition in the garden in winter.

Gardening as a competitive sport is a bit tough, especially when the only reason for being out there at all should be to get the logs in for the fire or to feed the birds. A winter garden should look good from the house windows, at a safe distance. It should not feature manky flowers. Several of our specialist gardens would fill this role nicely. Hedges and topiary, for example, look great outlined in hoar frost. Less so in snow, which blurs the outlines and makes things look a bit saggy – but most of us develop some fellow feeling for saggy over time. Ornamental grasses can be at their beautiful best for quite a lot of the winter. Meadows and lawns should be cut and satisfactorily flat and empty. Winter-flowering shrubs will irritate you by making you think you should go out and admire or smell them, a task you are unlikely to want to linger over. Much better to have shrubs, which do good things when you're going to pass them a lot because you are out there enjoying the spring or summer sunshine.

Perpetual winter would not be ideal, so the winter garden is really an optional extra. Making it your prime focus would be a bit Scrooge-like and fail to win you friends, but it would be original. There are 'Winter Gardens' to be found, to extend the garden visiting seasons of large punter-dependent gardens, and they tend to be full of all that is garish in winter – stems of coppiced willow and cornus in scarlet and orange, and lots of bright berries. It's terribly Walt Disney and makes you turn with relief to the delicate and beautiful browns and greens of the British countryside.

Whatever you do, don't dig.

DECKCHAIR WISDOM

Save your competitive instincts for playing
Monopoly by the fire with your family.
Best thing is to get both Mayfair and Park Lane
and build hotels.

Conclusion

My biggest message, perhaps, after all this, is be prepared to take advice, especially from me. And then be prepared to decide that as far as your garden is concerned, it's a load of old rubbish. Be sceptical of us all and be prepared to experiment, fail and then fail better.

Don't swallow all those 'things to do in your garden this week'. Go out and look; see for yourself what your garden may be needing. And make a garden that suits you, not one that fulfils the national stereotype.

It's very likely that you think I'm overstating the need for caution in taking expert advice in the garden. So I did a small experiment. I put the recommendations of one of our greatest garden pundits in front of Linda Chalker-Scott, who bases her horticultural advice on scientific testing. The results were shocking. The article was about plant tonics and supplements and its expert author had relied on questioning a variety of other experts for their best advice. Linda's first comment was 'It's full of inaccuracies (all nonsense).' I will spare you the long, detailed analysis but here are some of her comments.

Regarding blueing up hydrangeas with aluminium sulphate:

'A dangerous suggestion, especially if your garden is also used for food production. Aluminium is toxic. And bark mulch does not acidify soil.'

Or Epsom salts:

'Where would we be without Epsom salts for non-existent magnesium deficiencies? It's magical!!!' (This remark is sarcastic . . .)

The use of microorganisms and fungi to suppress harmful fungi and bacteria.

'*No demonstrated efficacy for this one. The inoculants are a marketing ploy. If you have access to decent soil, it has all the microbes you need. If you don't, go off site, get a handful of soil from a healthy ecosystem and use it to inoculate.*'

And so on. If you want to know more see the Facebook page 'The Garden Professors blog'. Linda is very happy to respond to queries there.

So how is it that we are so badly informed? There are several reasons. Linda suggests, 'I think it's because people think that gardening is just common sense. They don't understand that soil and plant sciences are academic fields of study, and many of them have no clue how plants work.' (That's me.)

Another reason is that garden experts are usually too busy filming, writing, and chatting on the radio to do science, and they would not have the resources or expertise to do science if they *had* got time. This includes me, you know – apart from the filming and radio.

Experts are also totally confident of their knowledge

– and able to be because gardens, soils and plants are very forgiving. Plants want to grow and will, with half a chance. So poor practice is rarely visible, and even if it were, there are so many variables that it's hard for an amateur or an expert to come to a sound conclusion about what the problem was.

You will have noted that I have not named the writer of the article that was subjected to the examination. That is because it is someone I know and like, who has been helpful and generous to me. The garden world is very small. People tend to know one another and not want to upset or challenge. And they don't want to be upset or challenged themselves, either.

And these experts are *loved*. In some cases, adored. The gardening public are in love with their TV and radio stars, magazine writers, and newspaper columnists. And the editors of all this media love them too. Why would they query the expertise? If the experts were exposed as fantasists the editors would lose their credibility along with them. And all this credulousness sticks.

Worse, anyone whose head emerges into the media light gets labelled an expert and is given instant credibility. No one knows what else to call them. I've been on national television described – erroneously – that way, alongside other 'experts' with no experience to speak of at all. And that can help you into print, you know.

And finally, horticulture is an industry and one that depends on selling to you. They also advertise alongside the material we're discussing, and that is an important consideration too for newspapers and magazines.

So if you have a garden problem, sure, you're going to Google it or ask an expert. But if you can restrain yourself for a minute, try contemplating the problem in the same way we're invited to consider our indoor clutter, KonMari style. Stand in front of whatever it is that is causing your problems, remember it at its best and ask yourself 'does this bring me joy?' If it is a plant, consider what you might treat yourself to instead. Would bunging it on the compost heap give you real joy – and relief – now? Do you really desperately need to grow your own kohlrabi? If it is an aspect of your garden, consider what a chainsaw or mini digger could do for you.

Address your garden in terms of problem solving, not following rules. When our cotoneasters began to die, I was reluctant to part with them altogether because they created a visual barrier between two parts of the garden. So I wondered if we could keep the dead branches – they were interesting, rather wild, sculptural shapes. We cleaned them up and left them there. Some people have admired them, and we found we like them. They now have ivy growing all over. I'm not sure if that works better or spoils the look. So, it becomes a new problem to solve. All the experts in the world aren't going to help you with that sort of thing, but imagination and an adventurous spirit might.

Every garden is different. Every garden owner is different. I'm a bit odd and I have a large garden in a wet part of the UK. You probably have little in common with me. So: grow your own way. And if in doubt – mulch.

Acknowledgements

I thought it might be useful and more entertaining than typical acknowledgements if I asked all these good people, who have generously helped me with the book, to tell you their best garden mistakes. So here they are, with my thanks to every one:

Charles Hawes

Going to great trouble to plant expensive trees in a wood where trees were naturally regenerating like weeds.

For a great subtitle and many helpful and not so helpful suggestions:

Katherine Crouch

Fondly believing that my nearest and dearest would share and support my plans for a beautiful garden . . . He so didn't – so now he isn't.

For doing the gardening that I don't want to:

Jeff Green

I had one guy working for me who said he knew his plants, so I put him on clearing a bed of weeds. He proceeded to remove everything. I stopped him halfway, had to replace the plants he'd binned and let him go at the end of the day, without pay.

For wise, knowledgeable and sympathetic help with the book-making process:

Sara Maitland

I don't think my gardening has ever risen to the level of catastrophic and/or entertaining blunders. It is always a bit of muddle through.

For enthusiastic support of everything involved, this lot:

Bridget Rosewell

Biggest mistake: thinking a *parterre* would work without too much effort. And I've made it twice (with a bit of help from a certain friend . . .)!

Example A – Santolina (cotton lavender) in the middle went leggy very quickly and looked awful.

Example B – *Ilex crenata* did not grow as expected and did not make a sensible low hedge.

Alice Hogge

I have lovingly tended a small sapling, given it the best and most expensive of tree guards to protect it from squirrels, ensured that the grass around it was kept short, and then . . . my vorpal blade went snicker-snack and I accidently secateured it in half in a fit of over-enthusiastic weeding.

Corinna Arnold

Worst mistake has probably been planting a willow hedge that is growing bushy and large and certainly doing its best to shield the veg patch from winds but also blocking sunlight from the greenhouse as it rises in height. V. basic mistake: not thinking of the eventual size and impact of a hedge!

Susan Wright

The worst mistake I made was not trusting my own judgement because I was frightened of making a mistake. So I was much too timid and probably made more mistakes than I would have done otherwise.

Jessica Hawes
Planting a Kiftsgate rose (can grow sixty feet or more) on an arch in a small town garden.

For getting me into this and then running away:

Hugh Barker
Never to plant a Russian vine again. And not to plant an apple tree on the one bit of lawn that turns out to have concrete foundations three feet down. (Which I only realized when the tree died and I dug it up again.)

For a gentle, understanding and sympathetic edit:

Gabriella Nemeth
I'm always guilty of buying beautiful plants that don't last more than two weeks because I've not considered whether I've got the right soil or if the spot is sunny/ shady enough for them.

Louise Dixon
I love wisteria. I buy them time and time again and plant them lovingly, always hoping for/expecting a beautiful display come flowering time. Only now, after years of trying, have I come to the conclusion that they hate me

and all I stand for. They hate my pots, they hate the wall I try to grow them up; they hate the fiddly bits of plastic wire I use to train them; the water I give them is too cold, too warm, not enough, too much. Will I try again? Probably.

And for the entertaining pictorial adventures of a certain gnome:

Kate Charlesworth

Apart from planting bulbs upside down and pruning out important bits of clematis, probably my greatest garden mistake was to get a puppy, who arrived qualified to degree level in chewing, digging and running away. The next mistake was to take her to our allotment – potentially worse than installing a hive of grumpy bees, which at least have a splendid horticultural function.